MW00337532

Copyright © 2021-All rights reserved.

No part of this publication may be reproduced, distributed, or transmitted in any form or by any means, including photocopying, recording, or other electronic or mechanical methods, without the prior written permission of the publisher, except in the case of brief quotations embodied in reviews and certain other non-commercial uses permitted by copyright law.

This Book is provided with the sole purpose of providing relevant information on a specific topic for which every reasonable effort has been made to ensure that it is both accurate and reasonable. Nevertheless, by purchasing this Book you consent to the fact that the author, as well as the publisher, are in no way experts on the topics contained herein, regardless of any claims as such that may be made within. It is recommended that you always consult a professional prior to undertaking any of the advice or techniques discussed with in.This is a legally binding declaration that is considered both valid and fair by both the Committee of Publishers Association and the American Bar Association and should be considered as legally binding within the United States.

CONTENTS

INTRODUCTION

The keto diet is a high-fat and low-carb diet that comes with various health benefits. It has been found that this diet can help you lose weight and improve the condition of your health. It might also show some positive effects on cancer, diabetes, Alzheimer's, and epilepsy. This diet's main aim is to reduce the intake of carbs drastically and replace the same with healthy fats. When you reduce the consumption of carbs, the body will enter a metabolic state known as ketosis. During ketosis, the body will try its best to burn the body fat for generating energy. It will also be turning the liver fat into ketones that supply energy to the brain.

A keto diet is a very effective way of losing weight. The best aspect of this diet is that you can lose bodyweight without counting calories. The reason behind this is that the diet will be so filling that you will not have frequent cravings. It has been found that people who follow a keto diet can lose 2.5 times more weight when compared to those people who follow a calorie-restrictive diet. The keto diet can also deal with type 2 diabetes, metabolic, and prediabetes syndrome. Some other benefits of the keto diet are:

• **Cancer:** This diet can help suppress the growth of tumors and might also help in treating various types of cancer.

• **Heart diseases:** The keto diet can help deal with various chronic heart conditions such as heart attack, stroke, and others.

• **Polycystic ovary:** This diet is well known for reducing insulin levels that can help in dealing with polycystic ovary.

There are certain food items that you will need to include while following this diet.

• **Fatty fish:** Trout, salmon, mackerel, tuna

• **Meat:** Steak, sausage, red meat, ham, chicken, bacon, turkey

• **Seeds and nuts:** Walnuts, almonds, pumpkin seeds, flax seeds, chia seeds

• **Oils:** Coconut oil, olive oil, avocado oil

A keto diet is an excellent option for all those who have diabetes, overweight or want to improve the health of their metabolism. I have included some tasty and easy keto recipes that you can include in your diet plan.

BREAKFAST & BRUNCH

Shakshuka

Ingredients for 2 servings
1 tsp olive oil
1 garlic clove, minced
1 small white onion, chopped
1 red bell pepper, chopped
1 small green chili, minced
1 cup diced tomatoes
½ cup tomato sauce
Salt and black pepper to taste
1 tsp cumin powder
1/3 cup baby kale, chopped
½ tsp dried basil
4 large eggs
¼ cup yogurt
½ lemon, juiced

Directions and Total Time: approx. 40 minutes
Heat olive oil in a deep skillet and sauté garlic, onion, bell pepper, and green chili until softened, 5 minutes. Stir in tomatoes, tomato sauce, salt, pepper, and cumin.
Cover and cook for 10 minutes. Add kale to wilt and stir in basil. Create four holes in the sauce with a wooden spoon, crack an egg into each hole, and sprinkle with parsley. Cover with a lid and cook until the eggs are firm, 8-10 minutes. In a bowl, mix yogurt with lemon juice and set aside. Plate shakshuka, top with a dollop of yogurt mixture, and serve.
Per serving: Cal 320; Net Carbs 8g; Fat 16.9g; Protein 17g

Gruyere Breakfast Soufflés

Ingredients for 4 servings
2 ½ cup Gruyere cheese, grated + a little extra for topping
2 egg whites, beaten until stiff
2 ½ tbsp butter, softened
2 ½ tbsp almond flour
1 ½ tsp mustard powder
½ cup almond milk
4 yolks, beaten

Directions and Total Time: approx. 20 minutes
Preheat oven to 370 F and brush the inner parts of 4 ramekins with butter. Melt the remaining butter in a pan over low heat and stir in flour for 1 minute. Remove from the heat, mix in mustard powder until evenly combined and slowly whisk in milk until no lumps form. Return to medium heat, while stirring until the sauce comes to a rolling boil. Stir in Gruyere cheese until melted. Into the egg yolks whisk ¼ cup of the warmed milk mixture, then combine with the remaining milk sauce. Fold in egg whites gradually until evenly combined. Spoon the mixture into the ramekins and top with the remaining cheese. Bake for 8 minutes, until the soufflés have a slight wobble, but soft at the center. Let cool and serve.
Per serving: Cal 488; Net Carbs 3.8g; Fat 39g; Protein 26g

Pumpkin Donuts

Ingredients for 4 servings
½ cup heavy cream
1 egg
2 egg yolks
½ tsp vanilla extract
2 tsp pumpkin pie spice
½ cup pumpkin puree
¼ cup sugar-free maple syrup
1 cup almond flour
¼ cup coconut flour
1 tsp baking powder
A pinch of salt
For the glaze:
2 cups swerve confectioner's sugar
4 tbsp water

Directions and Total Time: approx. 25 minutes
Preheat oven to 350 F. In a bowl, mix heavy cream, egg, egg yolks, vanilla extract, pie spice, pumpkin pie puree, and maple syrup. One after another, smoothly mix in almond and coconut flours, baking powder, and salt. Pour the batter into greased donut cups and bake for 18 minutes or until set. Remove, flip onto a wire rack and let cool. In a bowl, whisk the swerve and water until smooth. Swirl the glaze over the donut and enjoy immediately.
Per serving: Cal 189; Net Carbs 4.3g, Fat 16g, Protein 7.7g

Chorizo, Goat Cheese & Eggs

Ingredients for 4 servings
2 green onions, thinly sliced diagonally
1 tsp olive oil
1 tsp smoked paprika
3 oz chorizo, diced
4 eggs
½ cup crumbled goat cheese
2 tbsp fresh parsley, chopped

Directions and Total Time: approx. 15 minutes
Preheat oven to 350 F. In a pan, heat olive oil along with paprika for 30 seconds. Add the chorizo and cook until lightly browned; set aside. Crack the eggs into the pan, cook for 2 minutes, and then sprinkle with chorizo and crumble goat cheese all around the egg white, but not on the yolks. Transfer the pan to oven and bake for 2 more minutes, until the yolks are quite set, but still runny within. Garnish with green onions and parsley. Serve.
Per serving: Cal 257; Net Carbs 5.6g; Fat 18g; Protein 17g

Berries & Cream Bowl with Nuts

Ingredients for 6 servings

5 tbsp flax seed powder
1 cup dark chocolate
1 cup butter
1 pinch salt
1 tsp vanilla extract
2 cups fresh blueberries
4 tbsp lemon juice
1 tsp vanilla extract
2 cups coconut cream
4 oz walnuts, chopped
½ cup roasted coconut chips

Directions and Total Time: approx. 10 minutes

Preheat oven to 320 F. Line a springform pan with parchment paper. In a bowl, mix the flax seed powder with 2/3 cup water and allow thickening for 5 minutes. Break chocolate and butter into a bowl and microwave for 2 minutes. Share the flax egg into 2 bowls; whisk the salt into one portion and then, 1 tsp of vanilla into the other. Pour the chocolate mixture into the vanilla mixture and combine well. Fold into the other flax egg mixture. Pour the batter into the springform pan and bake for 20 minutes. When ready, slice the cake into squares and share into serving bowls. Pour blueberries, lemon juice, and remaining vanilla into a small bowl. Break the blueberries and let sit for a few minutes. Whip coconut cream with a whisk until a soft peak forms. To serve, spoon the cream on the cakes, top with blueberry mixture, and sprinkle with walnuts and coconut flakes.

Per serving: Cal 345; Fat 31g; Net Carbs 7g; Protein 6g

Coffee-Flavored Muffins

Ingredients for 4 servings
For the batter:
2 tbsp butter, softened
2 oz cream cheese, softened
1/3 cup sugar-free maple syrup
4 eggs
2 tsp vanilla extract
½ cup vanilla almond milk
1 cup almond flour
2 tsp instant coffee powder
½ cup coconut flour
1 tsp baking powder
For the topping:
1 cup almond flour
2 tbsp coconut flour
¼ cup swerve sugar
¼ cup butter softened
1 tsp cinnamon powder
½ tsp sugar-free maple syrup

Directions and Total Time: approx. 35 minutes

Preheat oven to 350 F and line a 12-cup muffin pan with paper liners. In a bowl, whisk butter, cream cheese, maple syrup, eggs, vanilla, and almond milk until smooth. In another bowl, mix almond flour, coffee powder, coconut flour, baking powder, and a pinch of salt. Combine both mixtures and fill the muffin cups two-thirds way up. In a bowl, mix flours, swerve, butter, cinnamon powder, and maple syrup. Spoon the mixture onto the muffin batter and bake for 25 minutes or until a toothpick inserted comes out clean. Remove from the oven, and let cool to serve.

Per serving: Cal 294; Net Carbs 5g, Fat 23g, Protein 17g

Pecan Cookies

Ingredients for 8 servings
1 egg
2 cups ground pecans
¼ cup sweetener
½ tsp baking soda
1 tbsp butter
20 pecan halves

Directions and Total Time: approx. 25 minutes

Preheat oven to 350 F. Mix the ingredients, except for the pecan halves, until combined. Make 20 balls out of the mixture and press them with your thumb onto a lined cookie sheet. Top each cookie with a pecan half. Bake for about 12 minutes. Serve warm or chilled.

Per serving: Cal 101; Net Carbs 0.6g; Fat 11g; Protein 2g

Cinnamon Faux Rice Pudding

Ingredients for 6 servings

1 ¼ cups coconut cream
1 tsp vanilla extract
1 tsp cinnamon powder
1 cup mashed tofu
2 oz fresh strawberries

Directions and Total Time: approx. 17 minutes

Pour coconut cream into a bowl and whisk until a soft peak forms. Mix in vanilla and cinnamon. Lightly fold in tofu and refrigerate for 10-15 minutes to set. Spoon into serving glasses, top with the strawberries and serve.

Per serving: Cal 225; Fat 20g; Net Carbs 3g; Protein 6g

Zucchini Muffins

Ingredients for 6 servings

½ cup almond flour
1 tsp baking powder
½ tsp baking soda
1 ½ tsp mustard powder
Salt and black pepper to taste
1/3 cup almond milk
1 large egg
5 tbsp olive oil
½ cup grated cheddar cheese
2 zucchinis, grated
6 green olives, sliced
1 spring onion, chopped
1 red bell pepper, chopped
1 tbsp freshly chopped thyme

Directions and Total Time: approx. 10 minutes

Preheat oven to 325 F. In a bowl, combine flour, baking powder, baking soda, mustard powder, salt, pepper. In a smaller bowl, whisk milk, egg, and olive oil. Mix the wet ingredients into dry ingredients and add cheese, zucchini, olives, spring onion, bell pepper, and thyme; mix well. Spoon the batter into greased muffin cups, and bake for 30 minutes or until golden brown. Let the muffins to cool.

Per serving: Cal 172; Net Carbs 1.6g; Fat 16g; Protein 4g

Chia Pudding with Blackberries

Ingredients for 2 servings
1 cup full-fat natural yogurt
2 tsp swerve
2 tbsp chia seeds
1 cup fresh blackberries
1 tbsp lemon zest
Mint leaves, to serve

Directions and Total Time: approx. 35 minutes
Mix together the yogurt and swerve. Stir in chia seeds. Reserve 4 blackberries for garnish and mash the remaining with a fork until pureed. Stir in the yogurt mixture. Refrigerate for 30 minutes. Divide the mixture into 2 glasses. Serve topped with raspberries and mint leaves.
Per serving: Cal 169, Net Carbs 1.7g, Fat 10g, Protein 7g

Lemon Muffins

Ingredients for 4 servings
For the muffins:
½ cup butter, softened
¾ cup swerve sugar
3 large eggs
1 lemon, zested and juiced
1 ½ cups almond flour
½ cup coconut flour
2 tsp baking powder
¼ tsp arrowroot starch
½ tsp vanilla extract
1 cup sour cream
A pinch of salt
For the topping:
3 tbsp butter, melted
¾ cup almond flour
3 Tbsp swerve sugar
1 tsp lemon zest
1 tbsp coconut flour
For the lemon glaze:
½ cup swerve confectioner's sugar
3 tbsp lemon juice
Directions and Total Time: approx. 35 minutes
For the muffins:
Preheat oven to 350 F and line a 12-cup muffin pan with paper liners. In a bowl, mix butter, swerve, eggs, lemon zest, and lemon juice until smooth. In another bowl, combine flours, baking powder, and arrowroot. Combine both mixtures and mix in vanilla, sour cream, and salt until smooth. Fill the cups two-thirds way up; set aside.
For the topping:
In a bowl, mix butter, almond flour, swerve, lemon zest, and coconut flour until well combined. Spoon the mixture onto the muffin batter and bake for 25 minutes or until a toothpick inserted comes out clean. Remove the muffins from the oven and cool while you prepare the glaze.
For the glaze:
In a bowl, whisk confectioner's sugar and lemon juice until smooth and semi-thick. Drizzle over the muffins.
Per serving: Cal 439; Net Carbs 7.6g; Fat 42g; Protein 8g

Yogurt Strawberry Pie with Basil

Ingredients for 4 servings
For the crust:
2 eggs
1 tsp vanilla extract
¼ cup erythritol
¼ tsp salt
1 cup almond flour
½ cup cold butter, cubed
5 tbsp cold water
1 tbsp olive oil
For the filling:
1 cup unsweetened strawberry jam
¼ cup heavy cream
1/3 cup erythritol
1 cup Greek yogurt
1 tbsp chopped basil leaves

Directions and Total Time: approx. 90 min + chilling time
For the piecrust:
In a bowl, whisk eggs, olive oil, and vanilla until well combined. In another bowl, mix erythritol, salt, and flour. Combine both mixtures into a stand mixer and blend until smooth dough forms. Add butter and mix until breadcrumb-like mixture forms. Add one tbsp of water, mix further until the dough begins to come together. Keep adding water until it sticks together. Lightly flour a working surface, turn the dough onto it, knead a few times until formed into a ball, and comes together smoothly. Divide into half and flatten each piece into a disk. Wrap each dough in plastic and refrigerate for 1 hour. Preheat oven to 375 F and grease a 9-inch pie pan with olive oil. Remove the dough from the fridge, let it stand at room temperature and roll one piece into 12-inch round. Fit this piece into the bottom and walls to the rim of the pie pan while shaping to take the pan's form. Roll out the other dough into an 11-inch round and set aside.
For the filling:
Whip the heavy cream and erythritol in a stand mixer until creamy and smooth. Mix in the Greek yogurt, strawberry jam, basil and mix on low speed until well combined. Fill the pie dough in the pie pan with the filling and level well. Brush the overhanging pastry with water and attach the top pastry on top of the filling. Press the edges to merge the dough ends and trim the overhanging ends to 1-inch. Fold the edge under itself and then, decoratively crimp. Cut 2 slits on the top crust. Bake the pie for 75 minutes until the bottom crust is golden and the filling bubbly.
Per serving: Cal 341; Net Carbs 6.1g; Fat 33g; Protein 5.6g

STARTERS & SALADS

Bruschetta with Tomato & Basil

Ingredients for 4 servings

3 ripe tomatoes, chopped
6 fresh basil leaves
5 tbsp olive oil
Salt to taste
4 slices zero carb bread, halved
1 garlic clove, halved

Directions and Total Time: approx. 1 hour 15 minutes

In a bowl, mix tomatoes and basil until combined. Drizzle with 2 tbsp olive oil and salt; do not stir. Set aside.

Brush bread slices with the remaining olive oil, arrange on a baking sheet, and place under the broiler. Cook for 2 minutes per side or until lightly browned. Transfer to a plate and rub garlic on both sides. Cover with tomato topping. Drizzle a little more of olive oil on top and serve.

Per serving: Cal 212; Net Carbs 2.7g; Fat 19g; Protein 8g

Speedy Beef Carpaccio

Ingredients for 4 servings

1 tbsp olive oil
½ lemon, juiced
Salt and black pepper to taste
¼ lb rare roast beef, sliced
1 ½ cups baby arugula
¼ cup grated Parmesan cheese

Directions and Total Time: approx. 10 minutes

In a bowl, whisk olive oil, lemon juice, salt, and pepper until well combined. Spread the beef on a large serving plate, top with arugula and drizzle the olive oil mixture on top. Sprinkle with grated Parmesan cheese and serve.

Per serving: Cal 106; Net Carbs 4.1g; Fat 5g; Protein 10g

Roasted Asparagus with Goat Cheese

Ingredients for 4 servings

1 lb asparagus, halved
2 tbsp olive oil
½ tsp dried tarragon
½ tsp dried oregano
½ tsp sesame seeds
1 tbsp sugar-free maple syrup
½ cup arugula
4 tbsp crumbled goat cheese
2 tbsp hazelnuts
1 lemon, cut into wedges

Directions and Total Time: approx. 30 minutes

Preheat oven to 350 F. Pour asparagus on a baking tray, drizzle with olive oil, tarragon, oregano, salt, pepper, and sesame seeds. Toss and roast for 15 minutes; remove and drizzle the maple syrup, and continue cooking for 5 minutes or until slightly charred. Spread arugula in a salad bowl and spoon the asparagus on top. Scatter with the goat cheese, hazelnuts, and serve with the lemon wedges.

Per serving: Cal 146; Net Carbs 3.4g; Fat 13g; Protein 4.4g

Savory Gruyere & Bacon Cake

Ingredients for 4 servings

½ cup shredded Gruyere cheese
4 eggs, eggs yolks and whites separated
2 tbsp butter
2 tbsp almond flour
1 cup heavy cream
6 slices bacon, chopped

Directions and Total Time: approx. 50 minutes

Melt butter in a pan over medium heat and mix in 1 tbsp of almond flour until well combined. Whisk in heavy cream, bring to a boil and while stirring, mix in the remaining almond flour until smooth. Turn the heat off. Cool the mixture for 3 minutes and slowly mix the batter into the egg yolks until well combined without cooking. Stir in Gruyere cheese until evenly distributed. Beat the egg whites in a mixer until stiff peak forms.

Fold the egg whites into the egg yolk mixture until well combined. Divide the mixture between 4 ramekins, top with bacon and bake in the oven for 35 minutes at 320 F.

Per serving: Cal 495; Net Carbs 2g, Fat 46g, Protein 17.3g

Warm Mushroom & Yellow Pepper Salad

Ingredients for 4 servings

1 cup mixed mushrooms, chopped
2 tbsp sesame oil
2 yellow bell peppers, sliced
1 garlic clove, minced
2 tbsp tamarind sauce
½ tsp hot sauce
1 tsp sugar-free maple syrup
½ tsp ginger paste
Salt and black pepper to taste
Chopped toasted pecans
Sesame seeds to garnish

Directions and Total Time: approx. 20 minutes

Heat half of the sesame oil in a skillet, sauté bell peppers and mushrooms for 8-10 minutes; season with salt and pepper. In a bowl, mix garlic, tamarind sauce, hot sauce, maple syrup, and ginger paste. Stir the mix into the vegetables and stir-fry for 2-3 minutes. Divide salad between 4 plates; drizzle with the remaining sesame oil and garnish with pecans and sesame seeds. Serve.

Per serving: Cal 289; Net Carbs 5.2g; Fat 27g; Protein 4.2g

Broccoli, Spinach & Feta Salad

Ingredients for 4 servings

2 tbsp olive oil
1 tbsp white wine vinegar
2 tbsp poppy seeds
Salt and black pepper to taste
2 cups broccoli slaw
2 cups chopped spinach
1/3 cup chopped walnuts
1/3 cup sunflower seeds
1/3 cup blueberries
2/3 cup chopped feta cheese

Directions and Total Time: approx. 15 minutes

In a bowl, whisk olive oil, vinegar, poppy seeds, salt, and pepper; set aside. In a salad bowl, combine the broccoli slaw, spinach, walnuts, sunflower seeds, blueberries, and feta cheese. Drizzle the dressing on top, toss, and serve.

Per serving: Cal 397; Net Carbs 4.9g; Fat 3.8g; Protein 9g

Tofu Pops

Ingredients for 4 servings
1 (14 oz) block tofu, cubed
1 bunch of chives, chopped
1 lemon, zested and juiced
12 slices bacon
12 mini skewers
1 tsp butter

Directions and Total Time: approx. 1 hour 17 minutes
Mix chives, lemon zest, and juice in a bowl and toss the tofu cubes in the mixture. Marinate for 1 hour. Remove the zest and chives off the cubes and wrap each tofu in a bacon slice; insert each skewer and the end of the bacon. Melt butter in a skillet and fry tofu skewers until the bacon browns and crisps. Serve with mayo dipping sauce.

Per serving: Cal 392; Net Carbs 9g, Fat 22g, Protein 18g

Blackberry Camembert Puffs

Ingredients for 4 servings
For the pastry cups:
¼ cup butter, cold and crumbled
¼ cup almond flour
3 tbsp coconut flour
½ tsp xanthan gum
½ tsp salt
4 tbsp cream cheese, softened
1/4 teaspoon cream of tartar
3 whole eggs, unbeaten
3 tbsp erythritol
1 ½ tsp vanilla extract
1 whole egg, beaten
For the filling:
5 oz Camembert, sliced and cut into 16 cubes
1 tsp butter
1 yellow onion, chopped
3 tbsp red wine
1 tbsp balsamic vinegar
5 tbsp erythritol
½ cup fresh blackberries
Freshly parsley to garnish

Directions and Total Time: approx. 30 minutes
Preheat oven to 350 F, turn a muffin tray upside down and lightly grease with cooking spray. In a bowl, mix almond and coconut flours, xanthan gum, and salt. Add in cream cheese, cream of tartar, and butter; mix with an electric hand mixer until crumbly. Stir in erythritol and vanilla extract until mixed. Then, pour in three eggs, one after another while mixing until formed into a ball. Flatten the dough on a clean flat surface, cover in plastic wrap, and refrigerate for 1 hour. Dust a clean flat surface with almond flour, unwrap the dough, and roll out the dough into a large rectangle. Cut into 16 squares and press each onto each muffin mound on the tray to form a bowl shape. Brush with the remaining eggs and bake for 10 minutes.

To make the filling, melt butter in a skillet and sauté onion for 3 minutes. Stir in red wine, balsamic vinegar, erythritol, and blackberries. Cook until the berries become jammy and wine reduces, 10 minutes. Set aside. Take out the tray and place a cheese cubes in each pastry. Return to oven and bake for 3 minutes. Spoon a tsp each of the blackberry sauce on top. Garnish with parsley to serve.

Per serving: Cal 372; Net Carbs 4.4g, Fat 32g, Protein 14g

Mini Ricotta Cakes

Ingredients for 4 servings

2 tbsp olive oil
2 tbsp butter
2 garlic cloves, minced
1 white onion, finely chopped
1 cup cauli rice
¼ cup white wine
¼ cup vegetable stock
2 scallions, chopped
Salt and black pepper to taste
¼ cup grated Parmesan
½ cup ricotta cheese
1 cup almond flour
½ cup golden flaxseed meal
2 eggs

Directions and Total Time: approx. 40 minutes

Heat butter in a saucepan over medium heat. Stir in garlic and onion and cook until fragrant and soft, 3 minutes. Mix in cauli rice for 30 seconds; add in wine, stir, allow reduction and absorption into cauli rice.

Mix in stock, scallions, salt, pepper, remaining butter, Parmesan and ricotta cheeses. Cover the pot and cook until the liquid reduces and the rice thickens. Open the lid, stir well, and spoon the mixture into a bowl to cool. Mold the dough into mini patties, about 14 to 16 and set aside. Heat olive oil in a skillet over medium heat; meanwhile pour the almond flour onto a plate, the golden flaxseed meal in another, and beat the eggs in a medium bowl. Lightly dredge each patty in the flour, then in eggs, and then coated accurately in the flaxseed meal. Fry in the oil until compacted and golden brown, 2 minutes on each side. Transfer to a paper towel-lined plate, plate, and garnish with some scallions.

Per serving: Cal 362; Net Carbs 6.2g, Fat 29g, Protein 13g

Mediterranean Roasted Turnip Bites

Ingredients for 4 servings

1 lb turnips, sliced into rounds
½ cup olive oil
2 garlic cloves, minced
1 tbsp chopped fresh parsley
2 tbsp chopped fresh oregano
3 tbsp dried Italian seasoning
¼ cup marinara sauce
¼ cup grated mozzarella

Directions and Total Time: approx. 1 hour

Preheat oven to 400 F. Place turnip slices into a bowl and toss with olive oil. Add in garlic, parsley, oregano, and Italian seasoning and mix well. Arrange on a greased baking sheet and roast for 25 minutes, flipping halfway. Remove and brush the marinara sauce. Sprinkle with mozzarella cheese and bake in the oven until the cheese is golden, 15 minutes. Garnish with parsley and serve warm.

Per serving: Cal 326; Net Carbs 3.8g; Fat 28g; Protein 5g

Cream Cheese & Caramelized Onion Dip

Ingredients for 4 servings

2 tbsp butter
3 yellow onions, thinly sliced
1 tsp swerve sugar
Salt to taste
¼ cup white wine
2 cups sour cream
8 oz cream cheese, softened
½ tbsp Worcestershire sauce

Directions and Total Time: approx. 30 minutes

Melt butter in a skillet and add in onions, swerve sugar, and salt and cook with frequent stirring for 10-15 minutes. Add in white wine, stir and allow sizzling out, 10 minutes.In a serving bowl, mix sour cream and cream cheese until well combined. Add onions and Worcestershire sauce; stir well into the cream. Serve with celery sticks.

Per serving: Cal 383; Net Carbs 8.3g; Fat 34g; Protein 8g

Tofu Jalapeño Peppers

Ingredients for 4 servings
For the poppers:
1 tbsp olive oil
4 oz firm tofu, chopped in bits
1 garlic clove, minced
½ cup cream cheese
1 lemon, zested juiced
4 scallions, finely chopped
2 tbsp chopped cilantro
Salt and black pepper to taste
6 jalapeño peppers, halved
3 tbsp grated cheddar cheese
For the dip:
1 tsp lemon juice
1 cup sour cream
1 tbsp chopped cilantro

Directions and Total Time: approx. 30 minutes
Preheat oven to 370 F. Heat olive oil in a skillet and fry tofu until golden. Transfer to a bowl. Mix in garlic, cream cheese, lemon zest, juice, scallions, cilantro, salt, and pepper. Arrange jalapeño peppers on a greased baking dish. Fill tofu mixture and sprinkle with cheddar cheese. Bake for 15 minutes or until the cheese is golden brown. In a bowl, mix lemon juice, sour cream, cilantro, and season with salt and pepper. Serve the dip with the poppers.
Per serving: Cal 247; Net Carbs 6.9g, Fat 21g, Protein 9g

Avocado Pate with Flaxseed Toasts

Ingredients for 4 servings
1/2 cup flaxseed meal
1 pinch salt
For the Avocado pate:
3 ripe avocado, chopped
4 tbsp Greek yogurt
2 tbsp chopped green onions
1 lemon, zested and juiced
Black pepper to taste
Smoked paprika to garnish

Directions and Total Time: approx. 5 minutes
For the flaxseed toasts:
Preheat oven to 350 F. Place a skillet over medium heat. Mix in flaxseed meal, 1/4 cup water, and salt and mix continually to form the dough into a ball. Place the dough between 2 parchment papers, put on a flat surface, and flatten thinly with a rolling pin. Remove the papers and cut the pastry into tortilla chips. Place on a baking sheet and bake for 8-12 minutes or until crispy. In a bowl, mix avocado, yogurt, green onions, lemon zest, juice, and black pepper until evenly combined. Spread the pate on the toasts and garnish with paprika. Serve immediately.
Per serving: Cal 364; Net Carbs 4g, Fat 31g, Protein 7.4g

Sweet Tahini Twists

Ingredients for 4 servings
For the puff pastry:
¼ cup almond flour
3 tbsp coconut flour
½ tsp xanthan gum
½ tsp salt
4 tbsp cream cheese, softened
¼ teaspoon cream of tartar
¼ cup butter, cold
3 whole eggs
3 tbsp erythritol
1 ½ tsp vanilla extract
1 whole egg, beaten
For the filling:
2 tbsp sugar-free maple syrup
3 tbsp tahini
2 tbsp sesame seeds
1 egg, beaten
2 tbsp poppy seeds

Directions and Total Time: approx. 15 min + cooling time

Preheat oven to 350 F and line a baking tray with parchment paper. In a bowl, mix almond and coconut flours, xanthan gum, and salt. Add in cream cheese, cream of tartar, and butter; mix with an electric mixer until crumbly. Add erythritol and vanilla extract until mixed. Then, pour in 3 eggs one after another while mixing until formed into a ball. Flatten the dough on a clean flat surface, cover in plastic wrap, and refrigerate for 1 hour.

Dust a clean flat surface with almond flour, unwrap the dough, and roll out the dough into a large rectangle. In a bowl, mix sugar-free maple syrup with tahini and spread the mixture over the pastry. Sprinkle with half of the sesame seeds and cut the dough into 16 thin strips. Fold each strip in half. Brush the top with the remaining egg, sprinkle with the remaining seeds, and poppy seeds. Twist the pastry three to four times into straws and place on the baking sheet. Bake until golden brown, 15 minutes. Serve with chocolate sauce.

Per serving: Cal 348; Net Carbs 3.1g, Fat 31g, Protein 11g

Feta Cheese Choux Buns

Ingredients for 4 servings

2 sprigs rosemary
6 tbsp butter
2/3 cup almond flour
3 eggs, beaten
1 tbsp olive oil
2 white onions, thinly sliced
2 tbsp red wine vinegar
1 tsp swerve brown sugar
1 cup crumbled feta cheese
½ cup heavy whipping cream

Directions and Total Time: approx. 40 minutes

Preheat oven to 350 F and line a baking tray with parchment paper. In a saucepan, warm 1 cup of water, salt, and butter melts. Bring to a boil and sift in flour, beating vigorously until ball forms. Turn the heat off; keep beating while adding the eggs, one at a time, until the dough is smooth and slightly thickened. Scoop mounds of the dough onto the baking dish. Press a hole in the center of each mound. Bake for 20 minutes until risen and golden. Remove from oven and pierce the sides of the buns with a toothpick. Return to oven and bake for 2 minutes until crispy. Set aside to cool.

Tear out the middle part of the bun (keep the torn out part) to create a hole in the bun for the cream filling. Set aside. Heat olive oil in a saucepan and sauté onions and rosemary for 2 minutes. Stir in swerve, vinegar, and cook to bubble for 3 minutes or until caramelized. In a bowl, beat whipping cream and feta together. Spoon the mixture into a piping bag and press a spoonful of the mixture into the buns. Cover with the torn out portion of pastry and top with onion relish to serve.

Per serving: Cal 384; Net Carbs 2.5g, Fat 37g, Protein 10g

SOUPS & STEWS

Brazilian Moqueca (Shrimp Stew)

Ingredients for 6 servings

1 ½ pounds shrimp, peeled and deveined
1 cup coconut milk
2 tbsp lime juice
¼ cup diced roasted peppers
3 tbsp olive oil
1 garlic clove, minced
14 ounces diced tomatoes
2 tbsp harissa sauce
1 chopped onion
¼ cup chopped cilantro
Salt and black pepper to taste

Directions and Total Time: approx. 25 minutes

Warm olive oil in a pot and sauté onion and garlic for 3 minutes. Add in tomatoes and shrimp. Cook for 3-4 minutes. Stir in harissa sauce, roasted peppers, and coconut milk and cook for 2 minutes. Add in lime juice and season with salt and pepper. Top with cilantro to serve.

Per serving: Cal 324; Net Carbs 5g; Fats 21g; Protein 23g

Yellow Squash Duck Breast Stew

Ingredients for 2 servings

1 pound duck breast, skin on and sliced
2 yellow squash, sliced
1 tbsp coconut oil
1 green onion bunch, chopped
1 carrot, chopped
2 green bell peppers, chopped
Salt and black pepper, to taste

Directions and Total Time: approx. 20 minutes

Set a pan over high heat and warm oil, stir in the green onions, and cook for 2 minutes. Place in the yellow squash, bell peppers, pepper, salt, and carrot, and cook for 10 minutes. Set another pan over high heat, add in duck slices and cook each side for 3 minutes. Pour the mixture into the vegetable pan. Cook for 3 minutes. Serve.

Per serving: Cal 433; Net Carbs 8g; Fat 21g, Protein 53g

Herby Chicken Stew

Ingredients for 6 servings
2 tbsp butter
2 shallots, finely chopped
2 garlic cloves, minced
1 cup chicken broth
1 tsp dried rosemary
1 tsp dried thyme
1 lb chicken breasts, cubed
1 celery, chopped
1 carrot, chopped
1 bay leaf
1 chili pepper, chopped
2 tomatoes, chopped
Salt black pepper to taste
½ tsp paprika

Directions and Total Time: approx. 60 minutes
Melt butter in a pot over medium heat. Add in shallots, garlic, celery, carrot, salt, and pepper and sauté until tender, about 5 minutes. Pour in chicken broth, rosemary, thyme, chicken breasts, bay leaf, tomatoes, paprika, and chili pepper; bring to a boil. Reduce the heat to low. Simmer for 50 minutes. Discard the bay leaf and adjust the seasoning. Serve warm.

Per serving: Cal 240; Net Carbs 5g; Fat 9.6g, Protein 245

South-American Shrimp Stew

Ingredients for 6 servings
1 cup coconut milk
2 tbsp lime juice
¼ cup diced roasted peppers
1 ½ lb shrimp, deveined
¼ cup olive oil
1 garlic clove, minced
14 ounces diced tomatoes
2 tbsp sriracha sauce
¼ cup chopped onions
¼ cup chopped cilantro
Fresh dill, chopped to garnish
Salt and black pepper to taste

Directions and Total Time: approx. 25 minutes
Heat olive oil in a pot and add cook onions and garlic for 3 minutes. Add in tomatoes, shrimp, and cilantro. Cook for about 3-4 minutes. Stir in sriracha and coconut milk, and cook for 2 more minutes. Do not bring to a boil. Stir in lime juice and season with salt and pepper. Spoon the stew in bowls, garnish with fresh dill, and serve.

Per serving: Cal 324; Net Carbs 5g; Fat 21g, Protein 23g

LUNCH & DINNER

Mushroom Pizza Bowls with Avocado

Ingredients for 4 servings
1 ½ cups cauli rice
2 tbsp water
Olive oil for brushing
2 cups pizza sauce
1 cup grated Monterey Jack
1 cup grated mozzarella
½ cup sliced mushrooms
2 large tomatoes, chopped
1 small red onion, chopped
1 tsp dried oregano
2 jalapeño peppers, chopped
Salt and black pepper to taste
1 avocado, chopped
¼ cup chopped cilantro

Directions and Total Time: approx. 40 minutes
Preheat oven to 400 F. Microwave cauli rice for 2 minutes. Fluff with a fork and set aside. Brush 4 ramekins with olive oil and spread half of pizza sauce at the bottom. Top with half of cauli rice and half of the cheeses. In a bowl, mix mushrooms, tomatoes, onions, oregano, jalapeños, salt, and pepper. Spoon half of the mixture into the ramekin and repeat the layering process, finishing off with cheese. Bake for 20 minutes. Top with avocados and cilantro.
Per serving: Cal 378; Net Carbs 3.4g; Fat 22g; Protein 21g

Pesto Tofu Zoodles

Ingredients for 4 servings
2/3 cup grated Pecorino Romano cheese
2 tbsp olive oil
1 white onion, chopped
1 garlic clove, minced
28 oz tofu, pressed and cubed
1 red bell pepper, sliced
6 zucchinis, spiralized
Salt and black pepper to taste
¼ cup basil pesto
½ cup shredded mozzarella
Toasted pine nuts to garnish

Directions and Total Time: approx. 20 minutes
Heat olive oil in a pot and sauté onion and garlic for 3 minutes. Add in tofu and cook until golden on all sides, then pour in the bell pepper and cook for 4 minutes. Mix in zucchinis, pour pesto on top, and season with salt and pepper. Cook for 3-4 minutes. Stir in the Pecorino cheese. Top with mozzarella, garnish with pine nuts, and serve.
Per serving: Cal 477; Net Carbs 5.4g; Fat 32g; Protein 20g

Veal Chops with Raspberry Sauce

Ingredients for 4 servings

3 tbsp olive oil
2 lb veal chops
Salt and black pepper to taste
2 cups raspberries
¼ cup water
1 ½ tbsp Italian Herb mix
3 tbsp balsamic vinegar
2 tsp Worcestershire sauce

Directions and Total Time: approx. 20 minutes

Heat oil in a skillet, season veal with salt and pepper and cook for 5 minutes on each side. Put on serving plates and reserve the pork drippings. Mash the raspberries in a bowl until jam-like. Pour into a saucepan, add water, and herb mix. Bring to boil on low heat for 4 minutes. Stir in veal drippings, vinegar, and Worcestershire sauce. Simmer for 1 minute. Spoon sauce over the veal chops and serve.

Per serving: Cal 413; Net Carbs 1.1g; Fat 32.5g; Protein 26g

Kale & Mushroom Pierogis

Ingredients for 4 servings

7 tbsp butter
2 garlic cloves, chopped
1 small red onion, chopped
3 oz bella mushrooms, sliced
2 oz fresh kale
Salt and black pepper to taste
½ cup cream cheese
2 cups Parmesan, grated
1 tbsp flax seed powder
½ cup almond flour
4 tbsp coconut flour
1 tsp baking powder

Directions and Total Time: approx. 45 minutes

Melt 2 tbsp of butter in a skillet and sauté garlic, red onion, mushrooms, and kale for 5 minutes. Season with salt and pepper and reduce the heat to low. Stir in cream cheese and ½ cup Parmesan; simmer for 1 minute. Set aside to cool. In a bowl, mix flax seed powder with 3 tbsp water and allow sitting for 5 minutes. In a another bowl, combine almond and coconut flours, salt, and baking powder. Put a pan over low heat and melt the remaining Parmesan and butter. Turn the heat off.

Pour the flax egg into the cream mixture, continue stirring, while adding the flour mixture until a firm dough forms. Mold the dough into four balls, place on a chopping board, and use a rolling pin to flatten each into ½ inch thin round pieces. Spread a generous amount of stuffing on one-half of each dough, then fold over the filling, and seal the dough with fingers. Brush with olive oil and bake for 20 minutes at 380 F. Serve.

Per serving: Cal 540; Net Carbs 6g; Fat 47g; Protein 18g

Cashew Quesadillas with Leafy Greens

Ingredients for 4 servings
3 tbsp flax seed powder
½ cup dairy-free cream cheese
1½ tsp psyllium husk powder
1 tbsp coconut flour
½ tsp salt
2 tbsp cashew butter
5 oz grated vegan cheddar
1 oz leafy greens

Directions and Total Time: approx. 30 minutes
Preheat oven to 400 F. In a bowl, mix flax seed powder with ½ cup water and allow sitting to thicken for 5 minutes. Whisk the cream cheese into the flax egg until the batter is smooth. In another bowl, combine psyllium husk, coconut flour, and salt. Add flour mixture to the flax egg batter and fold in until fully incorporated. Let sit for a few minutes. Line a baking sheet with parchment paper and pour in the mixture. Bake for 7 minutes until brown around the edges. Remove and slice into 8 pieces; set aside. Warm some cashew butter in a skillet and place a tortilla in the pan. Sprinkle with cheddar, leafy greens, and cover with another tortilla. Brown each side for 1 minute until the cheese melts. Repeat with the remaining cashew butter.
Per serving: Cal 470; Net Carbs 4g; Fat 40g; Protein 19g

BBQ Tofu Skewers with Squash Mash

Ingredients for 4 servings
7 tbsp fresh cilantro, chopped
4 tbsp fresh basil, chopped
2 garlic cloves
Juice of ½ a lemon
4 tbsp capers
2/3 cup olive oil
Salt and black pepper to taste
1 lb tofu, cubed
½ tbsp sugar-free BBQ sauce
½ cup vegan butter
3 cups butternut squash, cubed
2 oz grated vegan Parmesan

Directions and Total Time: approx. 30 minutes
In a blender, add cilantro, basil, garlic, lemon juice, capers, olive oil, salt, and pepper and process until smooth, 2 minutes. Set aside the salsa verde. Thread tofu cubes on wooden skewers. Season with salt and brush with BBQ sauce. Melt 1 tbsp vegan butter in a grill pan and fry tofu until browned on both sides; remove to a plate. Pour squash into a pot, add some salted water, and bring the vegetables to a boil for 15 minutes. Drain and pour the squash into a bowl. Add remaining vegan butter, vegan Parmesan cheese, salt, and pepper; mash vegetable. Serve tofu skewers with mashed squash and salsa verde.
Per serving: Cal 850; Net Carbs 5g; Fat 78g; Protein 26g

Roasted Chorizo & Mixed Greens

Ingredients for 4 servings

1 lb chorizo, cubed
1 lb asparagus, halved
2 mixed bell peppers, diced
1 cup green beans, trimmed
2 red onions, cut into wedges
1 head broccoli, cut into florets
Salt and black pepper to taste
4 tbsp olive oil
1 tbsp sugar-free maple syrup
1 lemon, juiced

Directions and Total Time: approx. 30 minutes

Preheat oven to 400 F. On a baking tray, add chorizo, asparagus, bell peppers, green beans, onions, and broccoli; season with salt, pepper, and drizzle with olive oil and maple syrup. Rub the seasoning onto the vegetables. Bake for 15 minutes. Drizzle with lemon juice and serve warm.

Per serving: Cal 300; Net Carbs 3.3g; Fat 18g; Protein 15g

Zoodle Bolognese

Ingredients for 4 servings

3 oz olive oil
1 white onion, chopped
1 garlic clove, minced
3 oz carrots, chopped
3 cups crumbled tofu
2 tbsp tomato paste
1 ½ cups crushed tomatoes
Salt and black pepper to taste
1 tbsp dried basil
1 tbsp Worcestershire sauce
2 lbs zucchini, spiralized
2 tbsp vegan butter

Directions and Total Time: approx. 45 minutes

Heat olive oil in a saucepan and sauté onion, garlic, and carrots for 3 minutes. Pour in tofu, tomato paste, tomatoes, salt, pepper, basil, some water, and Worcestershire sauce. Stir and cook for 15 minutes. Melt vegan butter in a skillet and toss in zoodles quickly, about 1 minute. Season with salt and pepper. Serve zoodles topped with the sauce.

Per serving: Cal 425; Net Carbs 6g; Fat 33g; Protein 20g

Baked Tofu with Roasted Peppers

Ingredients for 4 servings
3 oz dairy-free cream cheese
¾ cup vegan mayonnaise
2 oz cucumber, diced
1 large tomato, chopped
Salt and black pepper to taste
2 tsp dried parsley
4 orange bell peppers
2 ½ cups cubed tofu
1 tbsp melted vegan butter
1 tsp dried basil

Directions and Total Time: approx. 20 minutes
Preheat a broiler to 450 F and line a baking sheet with parchment paper. In a salad bowl, combine cream cheese, vegan mayonnaise, cucumber, tomato, salt, pepper, and parsley; refrigerate. Arrange bell peppers and tofu on the paper-lined baking sheet, drizzle with melted butter, and season with basil, salt, and pepper. Use hands to rub the ingredients until evenly coated. Bake for 15 minutes until the peppers have charred lightly and the tofu browned.
Per serving: Cal 840; Net Carbs 8g; Fat 76g; Protein 28g

Spicy Cheese with Tofu Balls

Ingredients for 4 servings
1/3 cup vegan mayonnaise
¼ cup pickled jalapenos
1 tsp paprika powder
1 tbsp mustard powder
1 pinch cayenne pepper
4 oz grated vegan cheddar
1 tbsp flax seed powder
2 ½ cup crumbled tofu
Salt and black pepper to taste
2 tbsp vegan butter, for frying

Directions and Total Time: approx. 40 minutes
In a bowl, mix mayonnaise, jalapenos, paprika, mustard, cayenne, and cheddar; set aside. In another bowl, combine flax seed powder with 3 tbsp water and allow absorbing for 5 minutes. Add the flax egg to the cheese mixture, crumbled tofu, salt, and pepper; mix well. Form meatballs out of the mix. Melt vegan butter in a skillet over medium heat and fry balls until cooked and browned on the outside.
Per serving: Cal 650; Net Carbs 2g; Fat 52g; Protein 43g

Zucchini Boats with Vegan Cheese

Ingredients for 2 servings
1 zucchini, halved
4 tbsp vegan butter
2 garlic cloves, minced
1½ oz baby kale
Salt and black pepper to taste
2 tbsp tomato sauce
1 cup vegan cheese
1 tbsp olive oil

Directions and Total Time: approx. 40 minutes
Preheat oven to 375 F. Scoop out zucchini pulp with a spoon. Keep the flesh. Grease a baking sheet with cooking spray and place the zucchini boats on top. Melt butter in a skillet and sauté garlic until fragrant and slightly browned, 4 minutes. Add in kale and zucchini pulp. Cook until the kale wilts; season with salt and pepper. Spoon tomato sauce into the boats and spread to coat evenly. Spoon kale mixture into the zucchinis and sprinkle with vegan cheese. Bake for 25 minutes. Drizzle with olive oil.
Per serving: Cal 620; Net Carbs 4g; Fat 57g; Protein 20g

Sweet & Spicy Brussel Sprout Stir-Fry

Ingredients for 4 servings
4 tbsp butter
4 shallots, chopped
1 tbsp apple cider vinegar
Salt and black pepper to taste
2 cups Brussels sprouts, halved
Hot chili sauce

Directions and Total Time: approx. 15 minutes
Melt half of butter in a saucepan over medium heat and sauté shallots for 2 minutes until slightly soften. Add in apple cider vinegar, salt, and pepper. Stir and reduce the heat to cook the shallots further with continuous stirring, about 5 minutes. Transfer to a plate. Pour Brussel sprouts into the saucepan and stir-fry with remaining vegan butter until softened. Season with salt and pepper, stir in the shallots and hot chili sauce, and heat for a few seconds.
Per serving: Cal 260; Net Carbs 7g; Fat 23g; Protein 3g

Roasted Butternut Squash with Chimichurri

Ingredients for 4 servings
Zest and juice of 1 lemon
½ red bell pepper, chopped
1 jalapeño pepper, chopped
1 cup olive oil
½ cup chopped fresh parsley
2 garlic cloves, minced
Salt and black pepper to taste
1 lb butternut squash
1 tbsp butter, melted
3 tbsp toasted pine nuts

Directions and Total Time: approx. 15 minutes
In a bowl, add lemon zest and juice, bell pepper, jalapeño, olive oil, parsley, garlic, salt, and pepper. Use an immersion blender to grind the ingredients until desired consistency is achieved; set chimichurri aside. Slice the squash into rounds and remove the seeds. Drizzle with butter and season with salt and pepper. Preheat grill pan over medium heat and cook the squash for 2 minutes on each side. Scatter pine nuts on top and serve with chimichurri.

Per serving: Cal 650; Net Carbs 6g; Fat 44g; Protein 55g

Tofu Eggplant Pizza

Ingredients for 4 servings
2 eggplants, sliced
1/3 cup melted butter
2 garlic cloves, minced
1 red onion
12 oz crumbled tofu
7 oz tomato sauce
Salt and black pepper to taste
½ tsp cinnamon powder
1 cup grated Parmesan
¼ cup chopped fresh oregano

Directions and Total Time: approx. 45 minutes
Preheat oven to 400 F and line a baking sheet with parchment paper. Brush eggplants with butter. Bake until lightly browned, 20 minutes. Heat the remaining butter in a skillet and sauté garlic and onion until fragrant and soft, about 3 minutes. Stir in tofu and cook for 3 minutes. Add tomato sauce and season with salt and pepper. Simmer for 10 minutes. Remove eggplants from the oven and spread the tofu sauce on top. Sprinkle with Parmesan cheese and oregano. Bake further for 10 minutes.

Per serving: Cal 600; Net Carbs 12g; Fat 46g; Protein 26g

Tomato Artichoke Pizza

Ingredients for 4 servings

2 oz canned artichokes, cut into wedges
2 tbsp flax seed powder
4¼ oz grated broccoli
6¼ oz grated Parmesan
½ tsp salt
2 tbsp tomato sauce
2 oz mozzarella cheese, grated
1 garlic clove, thinly sliced
1 tbsp dried oregano
Green olives for garnish

Directions and Total Time: approx. 40 minutes

Preheat oven to 350 F and line a baking sheet with parchment paper. In a bowl, mix flax seed powder and 6 tbsp water and allow thickening for 5 minutes. When the flax egg is ready, add broccoli, 4 ½ ounces of Parmesan cheese, salt, and stir to combine. Pour the mixture into the baking sheet and bake until the crust is lightly browned, 20 minutes. Remove from oven and spread tomato sauce on top, sprinkle with the remaining Parmesan and mozzarella cheeses, add artichokes and garlic. Spread oregano on top. Bake pizza for 10 minutes at 420 F. Garnish with olives.

Per serving: Cal 860; Net Carbs 10g; Fat 63g; Protein 55g

White Pizza with Mixed Mushrooms

Ingredients for 4 servings

2 tbsp flax seed powder
½ cup mayonnaise
¾ cup almond flour
1 tbsp psyllium husk powder
1 tsp baking powder
2 oz mixed mushrooms, sliced
1 tbsp basil pesto
2 tbsp olive oil
½ cup coconut cream
¾ cup grated Parmesan

Directions and Total Time: approx. 35 minutes

Preheat oven to 350 F. Combine flax seed powder with 6 tbsp water and allow sitting for 5 minutes. Whisk in mayonnaise, flour, psyllium husk, baking powder, and ½ tsp salt; let rest. Pour batter into a baking sheet.

Bake for 10 minutes. In a bowl, mix mushrooms with pesto, olive oil, salt, and pepper. Remove crust from the oven and spread coconut cream on top. Add the mushroom mixture and Parmesan. Bake the pizza further until the cheese melts, about 5-10 minutes. Slice and serve.

Per serving: Cal 750; Net Carbs 6g; Fat 69g; Protein 22g

Pepperoni Fat Head Pizza

Ingredients for 4 servings
3 ½ cups grated mozzarella
2 tbsp cream cheese, softened
2 eggs, beaten
1/3 cup almond flour
1 tsp dried oregano
½ cup sliced pepperoni

Directions and Total Time: approx. 35 minutes
Preheat oven to 420 F and line a round pizza pan with parchment paper. Microwave 2 cups of the mozzarella cheese and cream cheese for 1 minute. Mix in eggs and almond flour. Transfer the pizza "dough" onto a flat surface and knead until smooth. Spread it on the pizza pan. Bake for 6 minutes. Top with remaining mozzarella, oregano, and pepperoni. Bake for 15 minutes.
Per serving: Cal 229; Net Carbs 0.4g; Fats 7g; Protein 36.4g

Vegan Cordon Bleu Casserole

Ingredients for 4 servings
2 cups grilled tofu, cubed
1 cup smoked seitan, cubed
1 cup cream cheese
1 tbsp mustard powder
1 tbsp plain vinegar
1 ¼ cup grated cheddar
½ cup baby spinach
4 tbsp olive oil

Directions and Total Time: approx. 30 minutes
Preheat oven to 400 F. Mix cream cheese, mustard powder, plain vinegar, and cheddar in a baking dish. Top with tofu and seitan. Bake until the casserole is golden brown, about 20 minutes. Drizzle with olive oil.
Per serving: Cal 980; Net Carbs 6g; Fat 92g; Protein 30g

POULTRY

Savory Cheesy Chicken

Ingredients for 4 servings

1 ½ lb chicken breasts, halved lengthwise
½ cup sliced Pecorino Romano cheese
Salt and black pepper to taste
2 eggs
2 tbsp Italian seasoning
1 pinch red chili flakes
¼ cup fresh parsley, chopped
4 tbsp butter
2 garlic cloves, minced
2 cups crushed tomatoes
1 tbsp dried basil
½ lb sliced mozzarella cheese

Directions and Total Time: approx. 45 minutes

Preheat oven to 400 F. Season chicken with salt and pepper; set aside. In a bowl, whisk eggs with Italian seasoning and chili flakes. On a plate, combine Pecorino cheese with parsley. Melt butter in a skillet. Dip the chicken in the egg mixture and then dredge in the cheese mixture. Place in the butter and fry on both sides until the cheese melts and is golden brown, 10 minutes; set aside. Sauté garlic in the same pan and mix in tomatoes. Top with basil, salt, and pepper, and cook for 10 minutes. Pour the sauce into a greased baking dish. Lay the chicken pieces in the sauce and top with mozzarella. Bake for 15 minutes or until the cheese melts. Remove and serve with leafy green salad.

Per serving: Cal 674; Net Carbs 5.3g; Fat 43g; Protein 59g

Delicious Veggies & Chicken Casserole

Ingredients for 4 servings

¾ lb Brussels sprouts, halved
2 large zucchinis, chopped
2 red bell peppers, quartered
2 chicken breasts, cubed
¼ cup olive oil
1 tbsp balsamic vinegar
1 tsp chopped thyme leaves
1 tsp chopped rosemary
½ cup toasted walnuts

Directions and Total Time: approx. 30 minutes

Preheat oven to 400 F. Scatter Brussels sprouts, zucchinis, bell peppers, and chicken on a baking sheet. Season with salt and pepper, and drizzle with olive oil. Add balsamic vinegar and toss. Scatter thyme and rosemary on top. Bake for 25 minutes, shaking once. Top with walnuts and serve.

Per serving: Cal 485; Net Carbs 3.7g; Fat 34g; Protein 35g

Parsley Chicken & Cauliflower Stir-Fry

Ingredients for 4 servings
1 large head cauliflower, cut into florets
2 tbsp olive oil
2 chicken breasts, sliced
1 red bell pepper, diced
1 yellow bell pepper, diced
3 tbsp chicken broth
2 tbsp chopped parsley

Directions and Total Time: approx. 30 minutes
Heat olive oil in a skillet and season chicken with salt and pepper; cook until brown on all sides, 8 minutes. Transfer to a plate. Pour bell peppers into the pan and sauté until softened, 5 minutes. Add in cauliflower, broth, season to taste, and mix. Cover the pan and cook for 5 minutes or until cauliflower is tender. Mix in chicken, parsley. Serve.
Per serving: Cal 345; Net Carbs 3.5g; Fat 21g; Protein 32g

Baked Cheese Chicken

Ingredients for 6 servings
2 tbsp olive oil
8 oz cottage cheese, grated
1 lb ground chicken
1 cup buffalo sauce
1 cup ranch dressing
3 cups Monterey Jack, grated

Directions and Total Time: approx. 30 minutes
Preheat oven to 350 F. Warm oil in a skillet and brown chicken for a couple of minutes; set aside. Spread cottage cheese on a greased sheet, top with chicken, pour buffalo sauce, add ranch dressing, and sprinkle with Monterey cheese. Bake for 23 minutes. Serve with veggie sticks.
Per serving: Cal 216; Net Carbs 3g; Fat 16g; Protein 14g

Parsnip & Bacon Chicken Bake

Ingredients for 4 servings

6 bacon slices, chopped
2 tbsp butter
½ lb parsnips, diced
2 tbsp olive oil
1 lb ground chicken
2 tbsp butter
1 cup heavy cream
2 oz cream cheese, softened
1 ¼ cups grated Pepper Jack
¼ cup chopped scallions

Directions and Total Time: approx. 50 minutes

Preheat oven to 300 F. Put the bacon in a pot and fry on until brown and crispy, 7 minutes; set aside. Melt butter in a skillet and sauté parsnips until softened and lightly browned. Transfer to a greased baking sheet. Heat olive oil in the same pan and cook the chicken until no longer pink, 8 minutes. Spoon onto a plate and set aside too.

Add heavy cream, cream cheese, two-thirds of the Pepper Jack cheese, salt, and pepper to the pot. Melt the ingredients over medium heat, frequently stirring, 7 minutes. Spread the parsnips on the baking dish, top with chicken, pour the heavy cream mixture over, and scatter bacon and scallions. Sprinkle the remaining cheese on top and bake until the cheese melts and is golden, 30 minutes.

Per serving: Cal 757; Net Carbs 5.5g; Fat 66g; Protein 29g

Tasty Chicken Pot Pie with Vegetables

Ingredients for 4 servings

1/3 cup cremini mushrooms, sliced
3 tbsp butter
1 lb ground chicken
Salt and black pepper to taste
1 large yellow onion, chopped
2 baby zucchinis, chopped
1 cup green beans, chopped
½ cup chopped broccoli rabe
2 celery stalks, chopped
4 oz cream cheese
½ cup coconut cream
½ tsp dried rosemary
¼ tsp poultry seasoning
10 egg whites
4 tbsp coconut flour
2½ cups fine almond flour
2 tsp baking powder
½ cup shredded cheddar
6 tbsp butter

Directions and Total Time: approx. 60 minutes

Preheat oven to 350 F. Melt 1 tbsp of butter in a skillet, add chicken, season with salt and pepper, and cook for 8 minutes or until the chicken is no longer pink; set aside. Melt the remaining butter in the same skillet and sauté onion, zucchini, green beans, broccoli rabe, celery, and mushrooms. Cook until the vegetables soften, 5 minutes. Stir in chicken, cream cheese, and coconut cream. Simmer until the sauce thickens, 5 minutes. Season with rosemary and poultry seasoning and cook for 2 minutes. Turn the heat off and pour the mixture into a baking dish. Pour the egg whites into a bowl and using a hand mixer, beat the whites until frothy, but not stiff. Mix in coconut flour, almond flour, baking powder, cheddar, and salt until evenly combined. Beat the batter until smooth. Spoon the content in the baking dish and bake for 30 minutes or until the top browns. Remove from the oven and serve.

Per serving: Cal 808; Net Carbs 4.7g; Fat 68g; Protein 39g

Chili Pulled Chicken with Avocado

Ingredients for 4 servings
1 white onion, finely chopped
¼ cup chicken stock
3 tbsp coconut oil
3 tbsp tamari sauce
3 tbsp chili pepper
1 tbsp red wine vinegar
Salt and black pepper to taste
2 lb boneless chicken thighs
1 avocado, halved and pitted
½ lemon, juiced

Directions and Total Time: approx. 2 hours 30 minutes
In a pot, combine onion, stock, coconut oil, tamari sauce, chili, vinegar, salt, pepper. Add thighs, close the lid, and cook over low heat for 2 hours. Scoop avocado pulp into a bowl, add lemon juice, and mash the avocado into a puree; set aside. When the chicken is ready, open the lid and use two forks to shred it. Cook further for 15 minutes. Turn the heat off and mix in avocado. Serve with low carb tortillas.
Per serving: Cal 710; Net Carbs 4g; Fat 56g; Protein 40g

Savory Chicken Wings with Chimichurri

Ingredients for 4 servings
16 chicken wings, halved
Salt and black pepper to taste
½ cup butter, melted
3 garlic cloves, peeled
1 cup fresh parsley leaves
¼ cup fresh cilantro leaves
2 tbsp red wine vinegar
½ cup olive oil

Directions and Total Time: approx. 50 minutes
Preheat oven to 350 F. Put chicken in a bowl, season with salt and pepper, and pour butter all over. Toss to coat and transfer to a greased baking sheet. Bake for 40-45 minutes or until light brown and cooked within. Transfer to the same bowl. In a food processor, blend garlic, parsley, cilantro, salt, and pepper until smooth. Add in vinegar and gradually pour in olive oil while blending further. Pour the mixture (chimichurri) over the chicken; toss well to serve.
Per serving: Cal 603; Net Carbs 1.4g; Fat 54g; Protein 27g

Scallion & Saffron Chicken with Pasta

Ingredients for 4 servings

1 cup shredded mozzarella cheese
4 chicken breasts, cut into strips
1 egg yolk
3 tbsp butter
½ tsp ground saffron threads
1 yellow onion, chopped
2 garlic cloves, minced
1 tbsp almond flour
1 pinch cardamom powder
1 pinch cinnamon powder
1 cup heavy cream
1 cup chicken stock
¼ cup chopped scallions
3 tbsp chopped parsley

Directions and Total Time: approx. 35 min + chilling time

Microwave mozzarella cheese for 2 minutes. Take out the bowl and allow cooling for 1 minute. Mix in egg yolk until well-combined. Lay a parchment paper on a flat surface, pour the cheese mixture on top and cover with another parchment paper. Flatten the dough into 1/8-inch thickness. Take off the parchment paper and cut the dough into thick fettuccine strands. Place in a bowl and refrigerate overnight. Bring 2 cups of water to a boil and add the keto fettuccine. Cook for 1 minute and drain; set aside. Melt butter in a skillet, season the chicken with salt and pepper, and cook for 5 minutes. Stir in saffron, onion, and garlic and cook until the onion softens, 3 minutes. Stir in almond flour, cardamom powder, and cinnamon powder and cook for 1 minute.

Add in heavy cream and chicken stock and cook for 2-3 minutes. Mix in fettuccine and scallions. Garnish with parsley and serve warm.

Per serving: Cal 775; Net Carbs 3.1g; Fats 48g; Protein 73g

Spiralized Zucchini with Chicken & Pine Nuts

Ingredients for 4 servings
2 ½ lb chicken breast, cut into strips
5 garlic cloves, minced
¼ tsp pureed onion
Salt and black pepper to taste
2 tbsp avocado oil
3 large eggs, lightly beaten
¼ cup chicken broth
2 tbsp coconut aminos
1 tbsp white vinegar
½ cup chopped scallions
1 tsp red chili flakes
4 zucchinis, spiralized
½ cup toasted pine nuts

Directions and Total Time: approx. 30 minutes
In a bowl, combine half of garlic, onion, salt, and pepper. Add chicken and mix well. Heat avocado oil in a deep skillet over medium heat and add the chicken. Cook for 8 minutes until no longer pink with a slight brown crust. Transfer to a plate. Pour the eggs into the pan and scramble for 1 minute. Spoon the eggs to the side of the chicken and set aside. Reduce the heat to low and in a bowl, mix broth, coconut aminos, vinegar, scallions, remaining garlic, and chili flakes; simmer for 3 minutes. Stir in chicken, zucchini, and eggs. Cook for 1 minute and turn the heat off. Spoon into plates, top with pine nuts and serve warm.

Per serving: Cal 766; Net Carbs 3.3g; Fat 50g; Protein 71g

Lovely Pulled Chicken Egg Bites

Ingredients for 4 servings
2 tbsp butter
1 chicken breast
2 tbsp chopped green onions
½ tsp red chili flakes
12 eggs
¼ cup grated Monterey Jack

Directions and Total Time: approx. 30 minutes
Preheat oven to 400 F and line a 12-hole muffin tin with cupcake liners. Melt butter in a skillet, season chicken with salt and pepper, and cook it until brown on each side, 10 minutes. Transfer to a plate and shred with 2 forks. Divide between muffin holes along with green onions and chili flakes. Crack an egg into each muffin hole and scatter the cheese on top. Bake for 15 minutes until eggs set.

Per serving: Cal 393; Net Carbs 0.5g; Fat 27g; Protein 34g

Buffalo Spinach Chicken Sliders

Ingredients for 4 servings
4 zero carb hamburger buns, halved
3 lb chicken thighs, boneless and skinless
1 tsp onion powder
2 tsp garlic powder
Salt and black pepper to taste
2 tbsp ranch dressing mix
¼ cup white vinegar
2 tbsp hot sauce
½ cup chicken broth
¼ cup melted butter
¼ cup baby spinach
4 slices cheddar cheese

Directions and Total Time: approx. 3 hours 30 minutes
In a bowl, combine onion and garlic powders, salt, pepper, and ranch dressing mix. Rub the mixture onto chicken and place into a pot. In another bowl, mix vinegar, hot sauce, broth, and butter. Pour the mixture all over the chicken and cook on low heat for 3 hours. Using two forks, shred the chicken into small strands. Mix and adjust the taste. Divide the spinach in the bottom half of each low carb bun, spoon the chicken on top, and add a slice of cheddar cheese. Cover with the remaining bun halves and serve.
Per serving: Cal 774; Net Carbs 15.7g; Fat 37g; Protein 87g

Creamy Mustard Chicken with Shirataki

Ingredients for 4 servings
2 (8 oz) packs angel hair shirataki
4 chicken breasts, cut into strips
1 cup chopped mustard greens
1 yellow bell pepper, sliced
1 tbsp olive oil
1 yellow onion, finely sliced
1 garlic clove, minced
1 tbsp wholegrain mustard
5 tbsp heavy cream
1 tbsp chopped parsley

Directions and Total Time: approx. 30 minutes
Boil 2 cups of water in a medium pot. Strain the shirataki pasta and rinse well under hot running water. Allow proper draining and pour the shirataki pasta into the boiling water. Cook for 3 minutes and strain again. Place a dry skillet and stir-fry the shirataki pasta until visibly dry, 1-2 minutes; set aside. Heat olive oil in a skillet, season the chicken with salt and pepper and cook for 8-10 minutes; set aside. Stir in onion, bell pepper, and garlic and cook until softened, 5 minutes. Mix in mustard and heavy cream; simmer for 2 minutes and mix in the chicken and mustard greens for 2 minutes. Stir in shirataki pasta, garnish with parsley and serve.
Per serving: Cal 692; Net Carbs 15g; Fats 38g; Protein 65g

Jerk Chicken Drumsticks

Ingredients for 4 servings
½ cup Greek yogurt
2 tbsp melted butter
2 tbsp Jamaican seasoning
2 lb chicken drumsticks
3 tbsp pork rinds
¼ cup almond meal

Directions and Total Time: approx. 45 minutes
Preheat oven to 350 F. In a bowl, combine Greek yogurt, butter, Jamaican seasoning, salt, and pepper. Add the chicken and toss to coat evenly. Marinate for 15 minutes. In a food processor, blend the pork rinds with almond meal until well combined. Pour the mixture onto a wide plate. Remove chicken from the marinade, shake off any excess liquid, and coat generously in the pork rind mixture. Place on a greased baking sheet and bake for 30 minutes until golden brown and crispy, turning once. Serve warm.
Per serving: Cal 453; Net Carbs 1.8g; Fat 27g; Protein 45g

Creamy Chicken Thighs

Ingredients for 4 servings
1 pound chicken thighs
Salt and black pepper, to taste
1 tsp onion powder
¼ cup half-and-half
2 tbsp butter
2 tbsp sweet paprika

Directions and Total Time: approx. 50 minutes
In a bowl, combine paprika with onion, pepper, and salt. Season chicken pieces with this mixture and lay on a lined baking sheet; bake for 40 minutes in the oven at 400 F. Split the chicken in serving plates. Add the cooking juices to a skillet over medium heat, and mix with the half-and-half and butter. Cook for 6 minutes until the sauce thickens. Drizzle the sauce over the chicken and serve.
Per serving: Cal 381, Net Carbs 2.6g, Fat 33g, Protein 31g

Chicken Breasts with Jarred Pickle Juice

Ingredients for 4 servings

2 chicken breasts, cut into strips
4 oz chicken crisps, crushed
2 cups coconut oil
16 ounces jarred pickle juice
2 eggs, whisked

Directions and Total Time: approx. 30 min + chilling time

In a bowl, combine chicken with pickle juice; refrigerate for 12 hours. Place eggs in a bowl, and chicken crisps in a separate one. Dip the chicken pieces in the eggs, and then in chicken crisps until well coated. Set a pan and warm oil. Fry chicken for 3 minutes per side, remove to paper towels, drain the excess grease, and serve.

Per serving: Cal 387, Net Carbs 2.5g, Fat 16g, Protein 23g

Cream Cheese & Turkey Tortilla Rolls

Ingredients for 4 servings

10 canned pepperoncini peppers, sliced and drained
8 oz softened cream cheese
10 oz turkey pastrami, sliced

Directions and Total Time: approx. 2 hours 40 minutes

Lay a plastic wrap on a flat surface and arrange the pastrami all over, slightly overlapping each other. Spread the cheese on top of the salami layers and arrange the pepperoncini on top. Hold 2 opposite ends of the plastic wrap and roll the pastrami. Twist both ends to tighten and refrigerate for 2 hours. Slice into 2-inch pinwheels. Serve.

Per serving: Cal 266; Net Carbs 1g; Fat 24g; Protein 13g

Cucumber-Turkey Canapes

Ingredients for 6 servings

2 cucumbers, sliced
2 cups dices leftover turkey
¼ jalapeño pepper, minced
1 tbsp Dijon mustard
¼ cup mayonnaise
Salt and black pepper to taste

Directions and Total Time: approx. 5 minutes

Cut mid-level holes in cucumber slices with a knife and set aside. Combine turkey, jalapeno, mustard, mayonnaise, salt, and black pepper to be evenly mixed. Fill cucumber holes with turkey mixture and serve.

Per serving: Cal 170; Net Carbs 1.3g; Fat 14g; Protein 10g

Provolone Chicken Spinach Bake

Ingredients for 6 servings

1 ¼ cups provolone cheese, shredded
6 chicken breasts
1 tsp mixed spice seasoning
Salt and black pepper to taste
2 loose cups baby spinach
3 tsp olive oil
4 oz cream cheese, cubed

Directions and Total Time: approx. 45 minutes

Preheat oven to 370 F. Season chicken with spice mix, salt, and pepper. Put in a greased casserole dish and layer spinach over the chicken. Mix oil with cream cheese, provolone cheese, salt, and pepper and stir in 4 tbsp of water, one tbsp at a time. Pour the mixture over the chicken and cover the pot with aluminium foil. Bake for 20 minutes, remove foil and cook for 15 minutes. Serve.

Per serving: Cal 340, Net Carbs 3.1g, Fat 30g, Protein 15g

Italian Chicken-Basil Pizza

Ingredients for 4 servings

1 ½ cups grated mozzarella cheese
1 lb ground chicken
1 tsp Italian seasoning
1 cup tomato sauce
½ cup fresh basil leaves

Directions and Total Time: approx. 40 minutes

Preheat oven to 390 F and line a round pizza pan with parchment paper. In a bowl, mix ground chicken, Italian seasoning, and 1 cup of mozzarella cheese. Spread the pizza "dough" on the pizza pan and bake for 18 minutes. Spread tomato sauce on top. Scatter the mozzarella cheese and basil all over and bake for 15 minutes. Slice and serve.

Per serving: Cal 316; Net Carbs 0.4g; Fats 17g; Protein 35g

Tomato Basil Stuffed Chicken Breasts

Ingredients for 6 servings

4 ounces cream cheese

3 oz provolone cheese slices

10 ounces spinach

½ cup mozzarella, shredded

1 tbsp olive oil

1 cup tomato basil sauce

3 whole chicken breasts

Directions and Total Time: approx. 45 minutes

Preheat oven to 400 F. Microwave cream cheese, provolone cheese slices, and spinach for 2 minutes. Cut the chicken with the knife a couple of times horizontally. Stuff with the cheese filling. Brush the top with olive oil. Place on a lined baking dish and bake for 25 minutes. Pour the sauce over and top with mozzarella cheese. Return to oven and cook for 5 minutes. Serve.

Per serving: Cal 338, Net Carbs: 2.5g, Fat: 28g, Protein: 37g

Cranberry Glazed Chicken with Onions

Ingredients for 6 servings

4 green onions, chopped diagonally

4 tbsp unsweetened cranberry puree

2 lb chicken wings

2 tbsp olive oil

Chili sauce to taste

Juice from 1 lime

Directions and Total Time: approx. 50 minutes

Preheat the oven (broiler side) to 400 F. Then, in a bowl, mix the cranberry puree, olive oil, salt, sweet chili sauce, and lime juice. After, add in the wings and toss to coat. Place the chicken under the broiler, and cook for 45 minutes, turning once halfway. Remove the chicken after and serve warm with a cranberry puree and cheese dipping sauce. Top with green onions to serve.

Per serving: Cal 152, Net Carbs 1.6g, Fat 8.5g, Protein 17g

Acorn Squash Chicken Traybake

Ingredients for 4 servings

2 lb chicken thighs

1 lb acorn squash, cubed

½ cup black olives, pitted

¼ cup olive oil

5 garlic cloves, sliced

1 tbsp dried oregano

Directions and Total Time: approx. 60 minutes

Set oven to 400 F. Place the chicken with the skin down in a greased baking dish. Set garlic, olives and acorn squash around the chicken then drizzle with oil. Spread pepper, salt, and thyme over the mixture. Bake for 45 minutes.

Per serving: Cal: 411, Net Carbs: 5g, Fat: 15g, Protein: 31g

Turkey Bolognese Veggie Pasta

Ingredients for 6 servings

2 cups sliced mushrooms
2 tsp olive oil
1 pound ground turkey
3 tbsp pesto sauce
1 cup diced onion
2 cups sliced zucchini
6 cups veggie pasta, spiralized
Salt and black pepper to taste

Directions and Total Time: approx. 30 minutes

Heat oil in a skillet. Add turkey and cook until browned. Transfer to a plate. Add onions to the skillet, and cook until translucent, about 3 minutes. Add zucchini and mushrooms and cook for 7 more minutes. Return the turkey to skillet and stir in pesto sauce. Cover the pan, lower the heat, and simmer for 5 minutes. Serve immediately.

Per serving: Cal 273; Net Carbs 3.8g Fat 16g; Protein 19g

Grilled Garlic Chicken with Cauliflower

Ingredients for 6 servings

1 head cauliflower, cut into florets
3 tbsp smoked paprika
2 tsp garlic powder
1 tbsp olive oil
6 chicken breasts

Directions and Total Time: approx. 30 minutes

Place the cauliflower florets onto the steamer basket over boiling water and steam for approximately 8 minutes or until crisp-tender; set aside. Grease grill grate with cooking spray and preheat to 400 F. Combine paprika, salt, black pepper, and garlic powder in a bowl. Brush chicken with olive oil and sprinkle spice mixture over and massage with hands. Grill chicken for 7 minutes per side until well-cooked, and plate. Serve warm.

Per serving: Cal 422, Net Carbs 2g, Fat 35g, Protein 26g

Cucumber Salsa Topped Turkey Patties

Ingredients for 4 servings

2 spring onions, thinly sliced
1 pound ground turkey
1 egg
4 garlic cloves, minced
1 tbsp chopped herbs
2 tbsp ghee
1 tbsp apple cider vinegar
1 tbsp chopped dill
2 cucumbers, grated
1 cup sour cream
1 jalapeño pepper, minced
2 tbsp olive oil

Directions and Total Time: approx. 30 minutes

In a bowl, place spring onions, turkey, egg, two garlic cloves, and herbs; mix to combine. Make patties out of the mixture. Melt ghee in a skillet over medium heat. Cook the patties for 3 minutes per side. In a bowl, combine vinegar, dill, remaining garlic, cucumber, sour cream, jalapeño, and olive oil; toss well. Serve patties topped with salsa.

Per serving: Cal 475; Net Carbs 5g; Fat 38g; Protein 26g

Turkey with Avocado Sauce

Ingredients for 4 servings

1 avocado, pitted
½ cup mayonnaise
3 tbsp ghee
1 pound turkey breasts
1 cup chopped cilantro leaves
½ cup chicken broth

Directions and Total Time: approx. 25 minutes

Spoon avocado, mayo, and salt into a food processor and puree until smooth. Season with salt. Pour sauce into a jar and refrigerate.

Melt ghee in a skillet, fry turkey for 4 minutes on each side. Remove to a plate. Pour broth in the same skillet and add cilantro. Bring to a simmer for 15 minutes and add the turkey. Cook on low heat for 5 minutes until liquid reduces by half. Dish and spoon mayo-avocado sauce over.

Per serving: Cal 398, Net Carbs 4g, Fat 32g, Protein 24g

Bell Pepper Turkey Keto Carnitas

Ingredients for 4 servings

1 lb turkey breasts, sliced
1 garlic clove, minced
1 red onion, sliced
1 green chili, minced
2 tsp ground cumin
2 tbsp lime juice
1 tsp sweet paprika
2 tbsp olive oil
1 tsp ground coriander
1 green bell pepper, sliced
1 red bell pepper, sliced
1 tbsp fresh cilantro, chopped

Directions and Total Time: approx. 25 minutes

In a bowl, combine lime juice, cumin, garlic, coriander, paprika, salt, green chili, and pepper. Toss in the turkey pieces to coat well. Place a pan over medium heat and warm oil. Cook in turkey on each side, for 3 minutes; set aside. In the same pan, sauté bell peppers, cilantro, and onion for 6 minutes. Serve keto carnitas in lettuce leaves.

Per serving: Cal 262; Net Carbs 4.2g; Fat 15.2g; Protein 26g

Caprese Turkey Meatballs

Ingredients for 4 servings

2 tbsp chopped sun-dried tomatoes
1 pound ground turkey
2 tbsp chopped basil
½ tsp garlic powder
1 egg
¼ cup almond flour
2 tbsp olive oil
½ cup shredded mozzarella
Salt and black pepper to taste

Directions and Total Time: approx. 15 minutes

Place everything except for the oil in a bowl; mix well. Form 16 meatballs out of the mixture. Heat the olive oil in a skillet. Cook the meatballs for about 6 minutes. Serve.

Per serving: Cal 310; Net Carbs 2g; Fat 26g; Protein 22g

BEEF

Tangy Cabbage & Beef Bowl with Creamy Blue Cheese

Ingredients for 4 servings

3 tbsp butter
1 canon cabbage, shredded
1 tsp onion powder
1 tsp garlic powder
2 tsp dried oregano
1 tbsp red wine vinegar
1 ½ lb ground beef
1 cup coconut cream
¼ cup blue cheese
½ cup fresh parsley, chopped

Directions and Total Time: approx. 25 minutes

Melt 1 tbsp of butter in a deep skillet, and sauté cabbage, onion and garlic powders, oregano, salt, pepper, and vinegar, for 5 minutes; set aside. Melt the 2 tbsp butter in the skillet and cook the beef until browned, frequently stirring and breaking the lumps, 10 minutes. Stir in coconut cream and blue cheese until the cheese melts, 3 minutes. Return the cabbage mixture, and add parsley. Stir-fry for 2 minutes. Dish into serving bowls with low carb bread.

Per serving: Cal 542; Net Carbs 4.2g; Fat 41g; Protein 41g

Cheesy Tomato Beef Tart

Ingredients for 4 servings

2 tbsp olive oil
1 small brown onion, chopped
1 garlic clove, finely chopped
2 lb ground beef
1 tbsp Italian mixed herbs
4 tbsp tomato paste
4 tbsp coconut flour
¾ cup almond flour
4 tbsp flaxseeds
1 tsp baking powder
3 tbsp coconut oil, melted
1 egg
¼ cup ricotta, crumbled
¼ cup shredded cheddar

Directions and Total Time: approx. 1 hour 30 minutes

Preheat oven to 350 F. Line a pie dish with parchment paper and grease with cooking spray; set aside. Heat olive oil in a large skillet over medium heat; and sauté onion and garlic until softened. Add in beef and cook until brown. Season with herbs, salt, and pepper. Stir in tomato paste and ½ cup water, reduce the heat to low.

Simmer for 20 minutes; set aside. In a food processor, add the flours, flaxseeds, baking powder, a pinch of salt, coconut oil, egg, and 4 tbsp water. Mix starting on low speed to medium until evenly combined and dough is formed. Spread the dough in the pie pan and bake for 12 minutes. Remove and spread the meat filling on top. In a small bowl, mix ricotta and cheddar cheeses, and scatter on top. Bake until the cheeses melt and are golden brown on top, 35 minutes. Remove the pie, let cool for 3 minutes, slice, and serve with green salad and garlic vinaigrette.

Per serving: Cal 603; Net Carbs 2.3g; Fat 39g; Protein 57g

Olive & Pesto Beef Casserole with Goat Cheese

Ingredients for 4 servings
2 tbsp ghee
1 ½ lb ground beef
Salt and black pepper to taste
3 oz pitted green olives
5 oz goat cheese, crumbled
1 garlic clove, minced
3 oz basil pesto
1¼ cups coconut cream

Directions and Total Time: approx. 45 minutes
Preheat oven to 400 F and grease a casserole dish with cooking spray. Melt ghee in a deep, medium skillet, and cook the beef until brown; season to taste. Stir frequently. Spoon and spread the beef at the bottom of the casserole dish. Top with olives, goat cheese, and garlic. In a bowl, mix pesto and coconut cream and pour the mixture all over the beef. Bake until lightly brown around the edges and bubbly, 25 minutes. Serve with a leafy green salad.
Per serving: Cal 656; Net Carbs 4g; Fat 51g; Protein 47g

Maple Jalapeño Beef Plate

Ingredients for 4 servings
1 lb ribeye steak, sliced into ¼-inch strips
2 tsp sugar-free maple syrup
Salt and black pepper to taste
1 tbsp coconut flour
1/2 tsp xanthan gum
½ cup olive oil, for frying
1 tbsp coconut oil
1 tsp freshly pureed ginger
1 clove garlic, minced
1 red chili, minced
4 tbsp tamari sauce
1 tsp sesame oil
1 tsp fish sauce
2 tbsp white wine vinegar
1 tsp hot sauce
1 small bok choy, quartered
½ jalapeño, sliced into rings
1 tbsp toasted sesame seeds
1 scallion, chopped

Directions and Total Time: approx. 40 minutes
Season the beef with salt and pepper, and rub with coconut flour and xanthan gum; set aside. Heat olive oil in a skillet and fry the beef until brown on all sides. Heat coconut oil in a wok and sauté ginger, garlic, red chili, and bok choy for 5 minutes. Mix in tamari sauce, sesame oil, fish sauce, vinegar, hot sauce, and maple syrup; cook for 2 minutes. Add the beef and cook for 2 minutes. Spoon into bowls, top with jalapeños, scallion and sesame seeds. Serve.
Per serving: Cal 507; Net Carbs 2.9g; Fat 43g; Protein 25g

Cheese & Beef Avocado Boats

Ingredients for 4 servings

4 tbsp avocado oil
1 lb ground beef
Salt and black pepper to taste
1 tsp onion powder
1 tsp cumin powder
1 tsp garlic powder
2 tsp taco seasoning
2 tsp smoked paprika
1 cup raw pecans, chopped
1 tbsp hemp seeds, hulled
7 tbsp shredded Monterey Jack
2 avocados, halved and pitted
1 medium tomato, sliced
¼ cup shredded iceberg lettuce
4 tbsp sour cream
4 tbsp shredded Monterey Jack

Directions and Total Time: approx. 30 minutes

Heat half of avocado oil in a skillet and cook beef for 10 minutes. Season with salt, pepper, onion powder, cumin, garlic, taco seasoning, and paprika. Add the pecans and hemp seeds; stir-fry for 10 minutes. Fold in 3 tbsp Monterey Jack cheese to melt. Spoon the filling into avocado holes, top with 1-2 slices of tomatoes, some lettuce, a tbsp each of sour cream, and the remaining Monterey Jack cheese, and serve immediately.

Per serving: Cal 840; Net Carbs 4g; Fat 70g; Protein 42g

Morning Beef Bowl

Ingredients for 4 servings

1 lb beef sirloin, cut into strips
¼ cup tamari sauce
2 tbsp lemon juice
3 tsp garlic powder
1 tbsp swerve sugar
1 cup coconut oil
6 garlic cloves, minced
1 lb cauliflower rice
2 tbsp olive oil
4 large eggs
2 tbsp chopped scallions

Directions and Total Time: approx. 35 min + chilling time

In a bowl, mix tamari sauce, lemon juice, garlic powder, and swerve. Pour beef into a zipper bag and add in seasoning. Massage the meat to coat well. Refrigerate overnight. The next day, heat coconut oil in a wok, and fry the beef until the liquid evaporates and the meat cooks through, 12 minutes; set aside. Sauté garlic for 2 minutes. Mix in cauli rice until softened, 5 minutes. Season with salt and pepper; spoon into 4 serving bowls and set aside. Wipe the pan clean and heat 1 tbsp of olive oil. Crack in two eggs and fry sunshine-style, 1 minute. Place an egg on each cauliflower rice bowl and fry the other 2 eggs with the remaining olive oil. Serve garnished with scallions.

Per serving: Cal 908; Net Carbs 5.1g; Fat 83g; Protein 34g

Rosemary Beef Meatza

Ingredients for 4 servings

1 ½ lb ground beef
Salt and black pepper to taste
1 large egg
1 tsp rosemary
1 tsp thyme
3 garlic cloves, minced
1 tsp basil
½ tbsp oregano
¾ cup low-carb tomato sauce
¼ cup shredded Parmesan
1 cup shredded Pepper Jack
1 cup shredded mozzarella

Directions and Total Time: approx. 30 minutes

Preheat oven to 350 F and grease a pizza pan with cooking spray. In a bowl, combine beef, salt, pepper, egg, rosemary, thyme, garlic, basil, and oregano. Transfer the mixture into pan and using hands, flatten to a two-inch thickness. Bake for 15 minutes until the beef has a lightly brown crust. Remove and spread tomato sauce on top. Sprinkle with Parmesan, Pepper Jack, and mozzarella cheeses. Return to oven to bake until the cheeses melt, 5 minutes.

Per serving: Cal 319; Net Carbs 3.6g; Fat 10g; Protein 49g

Homemade Philly Cheesesteak in Omelet

Ingredients for 2 servings

4 large eggs
2 tbsp almond milk
2 tbsp olive oil
1 yellow onion, sliced
½ green bell pepper, sliced
¼ lb beef ribeye shaved steak
Salt and black pepper to taste
2 oz provolone cheese, sliced

Directions and Total Time: approx. 35 minutes

In a bowl, beat the eggs with milk. Heat half of the oil in a skillet and pour in half of the eggs. Fry until cooked on one side, flip, and cook until well done. Slide into a plate and fry the remaining eggs. Place them into another plate. Heat the remaining olive oil in the same skillet and sauté the onion and bell pepper for 5 minutes; set aside. Season beef with salt and pepper, and cook in the skillet until brown with no crust. Add onion and pepper back to the pan and cook for 1 minute. Lay provolone cheese in the omelet and top with the hot meat mixture. Roll the eggs and place back to the skillet to melt the cheese. Serve.

Per serving: Cal 497; Net Carbs 3.6g; Fat 36g; Protein 34g

Celery & Beef Stuffed Mushrooms

Ingredients for 4 servings

½ cup shredded Pecorino Romano cheese
2 tbsp olive oil
½ celery stalk, chopped
1 shallot, finely chopped
1 lb ground beef
2 tbsp mayonnaise
1 tsp Old Bay seasoning
½ tsp garlic powder
2 large eggs
4 caps Portobello mushrooms
1 tbsp flaxseed meal
2 tbsp shredded Parmesan
1 tbsp chopped parsley

Directions and Total Time: approx. 55 minutes

Preheat oven to 350 F. Heat olive oil in a skillet and sauté celery and shallot for 3 minutes. Transfer to a bowl. Add beef to the skillet and cook for 10 minutes; transfer to the bowl. Pour in mayo, Old Bay seasoning, garlic powder, Pecorino cheese, and crack in the eggs. Combine the mixture evenly. Arrange the mushrooms on a greased baking sheet and fill with the meat mixture. Combine flaxseed meal and Parmesan in a bowl, and sprinkle over the mushroom filling. Bake until the cheese melts, 30 minutes. Garnish with parsley to serve.

Per serving: Cal 375; Net Carbs 3.5g; Fat 22g; Protein 37g

Korean Braised Beef with Kelp Noodles

Ingredients for 4 servings

1 ½ lb sirloin steak, cut into strips
2 (16- oz) packs kelp noodles, thoroughly rinsed
1 tbsp coconut oil
2 pieces star anise
1 cinnamon stick
1 garlic clove, minced
1-inch ginger, grated
3 tbsp coconut aminos
2 tbsp swerve brown sugar
¼ cup red wine
4 cups beef broth
1 head napa cabbage, steamed
Scallions, thinly sliced

Directions and Total Time: approx. 2 hours 15 minutes

Heat oil in a pot over and sauté anise, cinnamon, garlic, and ginger until fragrant, 5 minutes. Add in beef, season with salt and pepper, and sear on both sides, 10 minutes.In a bowl, combine aminos, sugar, wine, and ¼ cup water. Pour the mixture into the pot, close the lid, and bring to a boil. Reduce the heat and simmer for 1 to 1 ½ hours or until the meat is tender. Strain the pot's content through a colander into a bowl and pour the braising liquid back into the pot. Discard cinnamon and anise and set aside. Add broth and simmer until hot, 10 minutes. Put kelp noodles in the broth and cook until softened and separated, 6 minutes. Spoon the noodles and some broth into bowls, add beef strips, and top with cabbage and scallions.

Per serving: Cal 548; Net Carbs 26.6g; Fat 27g; Protein 44g

Homemade Pasta with Meatballs

Ingredients for 4 servings

1 cup shredded mozzarella
1 egg yolk
½ cup olive oil
2 yellow onions, chopped
6 garlic cloves, minced
2 tbsp tomato paste
2 large tomatoes, chopped
¼ tsp saffron powder
2 cinnamon sticks
4 ½ cups chicken broth
Salt and black pepper to taste
2 cups pork rinds
1 lb ground beef
1 egg
¼ cup almond milk
¼ tsp nutmeg powder
1 tbsp smoked paprika
1 ½ tsp fresh ginger paste
1 tsp cumin powder
½ tsp cayenne pepper
½ tsp cloves powder
4 tbsp chopped cilantro
4 tbsp chopped scallions
4 tbsp chopped parsley
¼ cup almond flour
1 cup crumbled feta cheese

Directions and Total Time: approx. 1 hour + chilling time

Microwave mozzarella cheese for 2 minutes. Mix in egg yolk until combined. Lay parchment paper on a flat surface, pour the cheese mixture on top and cover with another piece of parchment paper. Flatten the dough into 1/8-inch thickness. Take off the parchment paper and cut the dough into spaghetti strands; refrigerate overnight. When ready, bring 2 cups of water to a boil in a saucepan and add the pasta. Cook for 1 minute, drain, and let cool. In a pot, heat 3 tbsp of olive oil and sauté onions and half of the garlic for 3 minutes. Stir in tomato paste, tomatoes, saffron, and cinnamon sticks; cook for 2 minutes. Mix in chicken broth, salt, and pepper. Simmer for 25 minutes.

In a bowl, mix pork rinds, beef, egg, almond milk, remaining garlic, salt, pepper, nutmeg, paprika, ginger, cumin, cayenne, cloves powder, cilantro, parsley, 3 tbsp of scallions, and almond flour. Form balls out of the mixture. Heat the remaining olive oil in a skillet and fry the meatballs for 10 minutes. Place them into the sauce and continue cooking for 5-10 minutes. Divide the pasta onto serving plates and spoon the meatballs with sauce on top. Garnish with feta cheese and scallions and serve.

Per serving: Cal 783; Net Carbs 6.3g; Fats 56g; Protein 55g

Mustard Beef Collard Rolls

Ingredients for 4 servings

2 lb corned beef
1 tbsp butter
Salt and black pepper to taste
2 tsp Worcestershire sauce
1 tsp Dijon mustard
1 tsp whole peppercorns
¼ tsp cloves
¼ tsp allspice
½ tsp red pepper flakes
1 large bay leaf
1 lemon, zested and juiced
¼ cup white wine
¼ cup freshly brewed coffee
2/3 tbsp swerve sugar
8 large Swiss collard leaves
1 medium red onion, sliced

Directions and Total Time: approx. 70 minutes

In a pot, add beef, butter, salt, pepper, Worcestershire sauce, mustard, peppercorns, cloves, allspice, flakes, bay leaf, lemon zest, lemon juice, wine, coffee, and swerve. Close the lid and cook over low heat for 1 hour. Ten minutes before the end, bring a pot of water to a boil, add collards with one slice of onion for 30 seconds and transfer to ice bath to blanch for 2-3 minutes. Remove, pat dry, and lay on a flat surface. Remove the meat from the pot, place on a cutting board, and slice. Divide meat onto the collards, top with onion slices, and roll the leaves. Serve with tomato gravy and pickled cabbages.

Per serving: Cal 349; Net Carbs 1.5g; Fat 16g; Protein 47g

Parsley Steak Bites with Shirataki Fettucine

Ingredients for 4 servings

2 (8 oz) packs shirataki fettuccine
1 lb thick-cut New York strip steaks, cut into 1-inch cubes
1 cup freshly grated Pecorino Romano cheese
4 tbsp butter
Salt and black pepper to taste
4 garlic cloves, minced
2 tbsp chopped fresh parsley

Directions and Total Time: approx. 30 minutes

Boil 2 cups of water in a pot. Strain the shirataki pasta and rinse well under hot running water. Allow proper draining and pour into the boiling water. Cook for 3 minutes and strain again. Place a dry skillet and stir-fry the shirataki pasta until visibly dry, 1-2 minutes; set aside. Melt butter in a skillet, season the steaks with salt and pepper, and cook for 10 minutes. Stir in garlic and cook for 1 minute. Mix in parsley and shirataki; toss and season with salt and pepper. Top with the Pecorino Romano cheese and serve.

Per serving: Cal 422; Net Carbs 7.3g; Fats 22g; Protein 36g

Cheddar Zucchini & Beef Mugs

Ingredients for 2 servings

4 oz roast beef deli slices, torn apart

3 tbsp sour cream

1 small zucchini, chopped

2 tbsp chopped green chilies

3 oz shredded cheddar cheese

Directions and Total Time: approx. 10 minutes

Divide the beef slices at the bottom of 2 wide mugs and spread 1 tbsp of sour cream. Top with 2 zucchini slices, season with salt and pepper, add green chilies, top with the remaining sour cream and then cheddar cheese. Place the mugs in the microwave for 1-2 minutes until the cheese melts. Remove the mugs, let cool for 1 minute, and serve.

Per serving: Cal 188; Net Carbs 3.7g; Fat 9g; Protein 18g

Classic Beef Ragu with Veggie Pasta

Ingredients for 4 servings

8 mixed bell peppers, spiralized

2 tbsp butter

1 lb ground beef

Salt and black pepper to taste

¼ cup tomato sauce

1 small red onion, spiralized

1 cup grated Parmesan cheese

Directions and Total Time: approx. 20 minutes

Heat the butter in a skillet and cook the beef until brown, 5 minutes. Season with salt and pepper. Stir in tomato sauce and cook for 10 minutes, until the sauce reduces by a quarter. Stir in bell peppers and onion noodles; cook for 1 minute. Top with Parmesan cheese and serve.

Per serving: Cal 451; Net Carbs 7.2g; Fats 25g; Protein 40g

Barbecued Beef Pizza

Ingredients for 4 servings

1 cup grated mozzarella cheese
1 ½ cups grated Gruyere cheese
1 lb ground beef
2 eggs, beaten
¼ cup sugar-free BBQ sauce
¼ cup sliced red onion
2 bacon slices, chopped
2 tbsp chopped parsley

Directions and Total Time: approx. 40 minutes

Preheat oven to 390 F and line a round pizza pan with parchment paper. Mix beef, mozzarella cheese and eggs, and salt. Spread the pizza "dough" on the pan and bake for 20 minutes. Spread BBQ sauce on top, scatter Gruyere cheese all over, followed by the red onion, and bacon slices. Bake for 15 minutes or until the cheese has melted and the back is crispy. Serve warm sprinkled with parsley.

Per serving: Cal 538; Net Carbs 0.4g; Fats 32g; Protein 56g

Beef with Parsnip Noodles

Ingredients for 4 servings

1 lb beef stew meat, cut into strips
1 cup sun-dried tomatoes in oil, chopped
1 cup shaved Parmesan cheese
3 tbsp butter
Salt and black pepper to taste
4 large parsnips, spiralized
4 garlic cloves, minced
1 ¼ cups heavy cream
¼ tsp dried basil
¼ tsp red chili flakes
2 tbsp chopped parsley

Directions and Total Time: approx. 35 minutes

Melt butter in a skillet and sauté the parsnips until softened, 5-7 minutes. Set aside. Season the beef with salt and pepper and add to the same skillet; cook until brown, and cooked within, 8-10 minutes. Stir in sun-dried tomatoes and garlic and cook until fragrant, 1 minute. Reduce the heat to low and stir in heavy cream and Parmesan cheese. Simmer until the cheese melts. Season with basil and red chili flakes. Fold in the parsnips until well coated and cook for 2 more minutes. Garnish with parsley and serve.

Per serving: Cal 596; Net Carbs 6.5g; Fats 35g; Protein 37g

Assorted Grilled Veggies & Beef Steaks

Ingredients for 4 servings

1 red and 1 green bell peppers, cut into strips
4 tbsp olive oil
1 ¼ pounds sirloin steaks
Salt and black pepper to taste
3 tbsp balsamic vinegar
½ lb asparagus, trimmed
1 eggplant, sliced
2 zucchinis, sliced
1 red onion, sliced

Directions and Total Time: approx. 30 minutes

Divide the meat and vegetables between 2 bowls. Mix salt, pepper, olive oil, and balsamic vinegar in a 2 bowl. Rub the beef all over with half of this mixture. Pour the remaining mixture over the vegetables. Preheat a grill pan. Drain the steaks and reserve the marinade. Sear the steaks on both sides for 10 minutes, flipping once halfway through; set aside. Pour the vegetables and marinade in the pan; and cook for 5 minutes, turning once. Serve.

Per serving: Cal 459; Net Carbs 4.5g; Fat 31g; Protein 32.8g

Classic Swedish Coconut Meatballs

Ingredients for 4 servings

1 ½ lb ground beef
2 tsp garlic powder
1 tsp onion powder
Salt and black pepper to taste
2 tbsp olive oil
2 tbsp butter
2 tbsp almond flour
1 cup beef broth
½ cup coconut cream
¼ freshly chopped dill
¼ cup chopped parsley

Directions and Total Time: approx. 30 minutes

Preheat oven to 400 F. In a bowl, combine beef, garlic powder, onion powder, salt, and pepper. Form meatballs from the mixture and place on a greased baking sheet. Drizzle with olive oil and bake until the meat cooks, 10-15 minutes. Remove the baking sheet. Melt butter in a saucepan and stir in almond flour until smooth. Gradually mix in broth, while stirring until thickened, 2 minutes. Stir in coconut cream and dill, simmer for 1 minute and stir in meatballs. Spoon the meatballs with sauce onto a serving platter and garnish with parsley. Serve immediately.

Per serving: Cal 459; Net Carbs 3.2g; Fat 32g; Protein 40g

Herbed Bolognese Sauce

Ingredients for 5 servings
1 pound ground beef
2 garlic cloves
1 onion, chopped
1 tsp oregano
1 tsp marjoram
1 tsp rosemary
7 oz canned chopped tomatoes
1 tbsp olive oil
Directions and Total Time: approx. 35 minutes
Heat olive oil in a saucepan. Cook onions and garlic for 3 minutes. Add beef and cook until browned, about 5 minutes. Stir in herbs and tomatoes. Cook for 15 minutes.
Per serving: Cal 318; Net Carbs 9g; Fat 20g; Protein 26g

Cheese & Beef Bake

Ingredients for 6 servings
2 lb ground beef
Salt and black pepper to taste
1 cup cauli rice
2 cups chopped cabbage
14 oz can diced tomatoes
1 cup shredded Gouda cheese
Directions and Total Time: approx. 30 minutes
Preheat oven to 370 F. Put beef in a pot, season with salt and pepper, and cook for 6 minutes. Add cauli rice, cabbage, tomatoes, and ¼ cup water. Stir and bring to boil for 5 minutes to thicken the sauce. Spoon the beef mixture into a greased baking dish. Sprinkle with cheese and bake for 15 minutes. Cool for 4 minutes and serve.
Per serving: Cal 385, Net Carbs 5g, Fat 25g, Protein 20g

Beef Burgers with Roasted Brussels Sprouts

Ingredients for 4 servings

1 ½ lb Brussels sprouts, halved

1 pound ground beef

1 egg

½ onion, chopped

1 tsp dried thyme

4 oz butter

Salt and black pepper to taste

Directions and Total Time: approx. 30 minutes

Combine beef, egg, onion, thyme, salt, and pepper in a mixing bowl. Create patties out of the mixture. Set a pan over medium heat, warm half of the butter, and fry the patties until browned. Remove to a plate and cover with aluminium foil. Fry Brussels sprouts in the remaining butter, season to taste, then set into a bowl. Plate the burgers and Brussels sprouts and serve.

Per serving: Cal: 443, Net Carbs: 5g, Fat: 25g, Protein: 31g

Easy Rump Steak Salad

Ingredients for 4 servings

1 pound flank steak

½ pound Brussels sprouts

3 green onions, sliced

1 cucumber, sliced

1 cup green beans, sliced

9 oz mixed salad greens

Salad Dressing

2 tsp Dijon mustard

1 tsp xylitol

3 tbsp extra virgin olive oil

1 tbsp red wine vinegar

Directions and Total Time: approx. 40 minutes

Preheat a grill pan, season the meat with salt and pepper, and brown the steak for 5 minutes per side. Remove to a chopping board and slice thinly. Put Brussels sprouts on a baking sheet, drizzle with olive oil and bake for 25 minutes at 400 F; set aside. In a bowl, mix mustard, xylitol, salt, pepper, vinegar, and olive oil. Set aside. In a shallow salad bowl, add green onions, cucumber, green beans, cooled Brussels sprouts, salad greens, and steak slices. Serve.

Per serving: Cal 244; Net Carbs 3.3g; Fat 11g; Protein 27.4g

Garlicky Roast Rib of Beef

Ingredients for 6 servings
4 tbsp olive oil
3 pounds beef ribs
3 heads garlic, cut in half
3 onions, halved
2 lemons, zested
A pinch of mustard powder
3 tbsp xylitol
Salt and black pepper to taste
3 tbsp fresh sage leaves
¼ cup red wine

Directions and Total Time: approx. 55 minutes
Score shallow crisscrosses patterns on the meat. Mix xylitol, mustard powder, sage, salt, pepper, and lemon zest to make a rub; and apply it all over the beef with your hands, particularly into the cuts. Place garlic heads and onion halves in a baking dish, toss with olive oil, and bake for 15 minutes at 410 F. Place beef on top of the onion and garlic. Pour in ¼ cup water and red wine, cover the dish with foil and bake for 15 minutes. Remove the foil and bake for 10 minutes. Let cool and slice. Serve warm.

Per serving: Cal 749; Net Carbs 5.5g; Fat 65.6g; Protein 53g

Spicy Cheese & Kale Pinwheel

Ingredients for 4 servings
2 tbsp olive oil
1 pound flank steak
1 cup cotija cheese, crumbled
1 cup kale
1 habanero pepper, chopped
2 tbsp cilantro, chopped

Directions and Total Time: approx. 42 minutes
Cover the meat with plastic wrap on a flat surface and flatten with a mallet. Take off the wraps. Sprinkle with half of the cheese, top with kale, habanero pepper, cilantro, and the remaining cheese. Roll the steak over on the stuffing and secure with toothpicks. Place in a greased baking sheet and cook for 30 minutes at 400 F, flipping once. Cool for 3 minutes and slice into pinwheels to serve.

Per serving: Cal 349; Net Carbs 2.2g; Fat 22.5g; Protein 33g

Beef Stuffed Zucchini Boats

Ingredients for 4 servings

4 zucchinis
2 tbsp olive oil
1 ½ lb ground beef
1 medium red onion, chopped
2 tbsp chopped pimiento
1 cup Colby cheese, grated

Directions and Total Time: approx. 45 minutes

Preheat oven to 350 F. Lay the zucchinis on a flat surface, trim off the ends and cut in half lengthwise. Scoop out pulp from each half with a spoon to make shells. Chop the pulp. Heat oil in a skillet; add the ground beef, red onion, pimiento, and zucchini pulp, and season with salt and black pepper. Cook for 6 minutes. Spoon the beef into the boats and sprinkle with colby cheese. Place on a greased baking sheet and cook for 15 minutes. Serve warm.

Per serving: Cal 335, Net Carbs 7g, Fat 24g, Protein 18g

Pickled Peppers & Beef Salad with Feta

Ingredients for 4 servings

1 lb skirt steak, sliced
Salt and black pepper to taste
1 taste olive oil
4 radishes, sliced
1 ½ cups mixed salad greens
3 chopped pickled peppers
2 tbsp red wine vinaigrette
½ cup feta cheese, crumbled

Directions and Total Time: approx. 15 minutes

Brush steaks with olive oil and season with salt and pepper. Heat a pan and cook steaks for about 5-6 minutes. Remove to a bowl, cover and leave to rest while you make the salad. Mix the salad greens, radishes, pickled peppers, and vinaigrette in a salad bowl. Add the beef and sprinkle with cheese. Serve the salad with roasted parsnips.

Per serving: Cal 315, Net Carbs 2g, Fat 26g, Protein 18g

Beef Stir-Fry with Peanut Sauce

Ingredients for 4 servings

2 cups mixed vegetables
1 ½ tbsp ghee
2 lb beef loin, cut into strips
Salt and chili pepper to taste
2 tsp ginger-garlic paste
¼ cup chicken broth
5 tbsp peanut butter

Directions and Total Time: approx. 30 minutes

Melt ghee in a wok. Season the beef with salt, chili pepper, and ginger-garlic paste. Pour the beef into the wok and cook for 6 minutes until no longer pink. In a small bowl, mix the peanut butter with some broth, add to the beef and stir; cook for 2 minutes. Pour in the remaining broth, cook for 4 minutes, and add the mixed veggies. Simmer for 5 minutes. Adjust the taste with salt and pepper and serve.

Per serving: Cal 571, Net Carbs 1g, Fat 49g, Protein 22.5g

Rosemary Creamy Beef

Ingredients for 4 servings

1 tbsp olive oil
3 tbsp butter
2 tbsp rosemary, chopped
1 tbsp garlic powder
4 beef steaks
1 red onion, chopped
½ cup half-and-half
½ cup beef stock
1 tbsp mustard
2 tsp lemon juice
A sprig of sage
A sprig of thyme

Directions and Total Time: approx. 25 minutes

Rub olive oil, garlic powder, and chopped rosemary all over the steaks slices and season with salt and pepper. Heat butter in a pan, place in beef steaks, and cook for 6 minutes, flipping once; set aside. In the same pan, add red onion and cook for 3 minutes; stir in beef stock, thyme sprig, half-and-half, mustard, and sage sprig, and cook for 8 minutes. Stir in lemon juice, pepper, and salt. Remove sage and thyme sprigs. Sprinkle with rosemary to serve.

Per serving: Cal 481; Net Carbs 7.8g; Fat 25g; Protein 51.7g

Steak Carnitas

Ingredients for 4 servings

2 lb sirloin steak, cut into strips
2 tbsp Cajun seasoning
4 oz guacamole
Salt to taste
2 tbsp olive oil
2 shallots, sliced
1 red bell pepper, sliced
8 low carb tortillas

Directions and Total Time: approx. 35 minutes

Preheat grill to 425 F. Rub the steaks all over with Cajun seasoning and place in the fridge for 1 hour. Grill the steaks for 6 minutes per side, flipping once. Wrap in foil and let sit for 10 minutes. Heat olive oil in a skillet and sauté shallots and bell pepper for 5 minutes. Share the strips in the tortillas and top with veggies and guacamole.

Per serving: Cal 381; Net Carbs 5g; Fat 16.7g; Protein 47g

Tasty Beef Cheeseburgers

Ingredients for 4 servings

1 lb ground beef
1 tsp dried parsley
½ tsp Worcestershire sauce
Salt and black pepper to taste
1 cup feta cheese, shredded
4 zero carb buns, halved

Directions and Total Time: approx. 20 minutes

Preheat grill to 400 F and grease the grate with cooking spray. Mix beef, parsley, Worcestershire sauce, salt, and pepper with until evenly combined. Make patties out of the mixture. Cook on the grill for 7 minutes one side. Flip the patties and top with cheese. Cook for another 7 minutes. Remove the patties and sandwich into 2 halves of a bun each. Serve with a tomato dipping sauce.

Per serving: Cal 386, Net Carbs 2g, Fat 32g, Protein 21g

Beef & Pesto Filled Tomatoes

Ingredients for 6 servings

1 tbsp olive oil
¼ lb ground beef
Salt and black pepper to taste
4 medium tomatoes, halved
4 tsp basil pesto
5 tbsp shredded Parmesan

Directions and Total Time: approx. 30 minutes

Preheat oven to 400 F. Heat olive oil in a skillet, add in beef, season with salt and pepper, and cook until brown while breaking the lumps that form, 8 minutes. Remove the seeds of tomatoes to create a cavity and spoon the beef inside them. Top with pesto and Parmesan. Place the filled tomatoes on a greased baking sheet and bake until the cheese melts and the tomatoes slightly brown, 20 minutes.

Per serving: Cal 122; Net Carbs 2.9g; Fat 4.4g; Protein 7.3g

Habanero Beef Cauliflower Pilaf

Ingredients for 4 servings

3 tbsp olive oil
½ lb ground beef
Salt and black pepper to taste
1 yellow onion, chopped
3 garlic cloves, minced
1 habanero pepper, minced
½ tsp Italian seasoning
2 ½ cups cauliflower rice
2 tbsp tomato paste
½ cup beef broth
¼ cup chopped parsley
1 lemon, sliced

Directions and Total Time: approx. 30 minutes

Heat olive oil in a skillet over medium heat and cook the beef until no longer brown, 8 minutes. Season with salt and pepper and spoon into a serving plate. In the same skillet, sauté onion, garlic, and habanero pepper, 2 minutes. Mix in Italian seasoning. Stir in cauli rice, tomato paste, and broth. Season to taste, and cook covered for 10 minutes. Mix in beef for 3 minutes. Garnish with parsley to serve.

Per serving: Cal 216; Net Carbs 3.8g; Fat 14g; Protein 15g

Beef Patties with Cherry Tomatoes

Ingredients for 4 servings

2 slices cheddar cheese, cut into 4 pieces each
2 pearl onions, thinly sliced into 8 pieces
½ lb ground beef
1 tsp garlic powder
1 tsp onion powder
8 slices zero carb bread
2 tbsp ranch dressing
4 cherry tomatoes, halved

Directions and Total Time: approx. 30 minutes

Preheat oven to 400 F. In a bowl, combine beef, salt, pepper, garlic and onion powders. Form 8 patties and place them on a greased baking sheet. Bake until brown and cooked, 10 minutes. Let cool for 3 minutes. Cut out 16 circles from the bread slices. Lay half of the bread circles on clean, flat surface and brush with the ranch dressing. Place the meat patties on the bread slices, divide cheese slices on top, onions, and tomatoes. Cover with the remaining bread slices and secure with a toothpick. Serve.

Per serving: Cal 281; Net Carbs 2.8g; Fat 12g; Protein 20g

PORK

Mushroom Pork Meatballs with Parsnips

Ingredients for 4 servings

1 cup cremini mushrooms, chopped
1 ½ lb ground pork
2 garlic cloves, minced
2 small red onions, chopped
1 tsp dried basil
Salt and black pepper to taste
1 cup grated Parmesan
½ almond milk
2 tbsp olive oil
2 cups tomato sauce
6 fresh basil leaves to garnish
1 lb parsnips, chopped
1 cup water
2 tbsp butter
½ cup coconut cream

Directions and Total Time: approx. 60 minutes

Preheat oven to 350 F and line a baking tray with parchment paper. In a bowl, add pork, half of garlic, half of onion, mushrooms, basil, salt, and pepper; mix with hands until evenly combined. Mold bite-size balls out of the mixture. Pour ½ cup Parmesan and almond milk each in 2 separate bowls. Dip each ball in the milk and then in the cheese. Place on the tray and bake for 20 minutes.

Heat olive oil in a saucepan and sauté the remaining onion and garlic; sauté until fragrant and soft. Pour in tomato sauce and cook for 20 minutes. Add the meatballs, spoon some sauce to cover, and simmer for 7 minutes. In a pot, add parsnips, 1 cup water, and salt. Bring to a boil for 10 minutes until the parsnips soften. Drain and pour into a bowl. Add butter, salt, and pepper; mash into a puree using a mash. Stir in coconut cream and remaining Parmesan until combined. Spoon mashed parsnip into bowls, top with meatballs and sauce, and garnish with basil leaves.

Per serving: Cal 642; Net Carbs 21.1g; Fat 32g; Protein 50g

Smoked Paprika-Coconut Tenderloin

Ingredients for 4 servings

1 lb pork tenderloin, cubed
4 tsp smoked paprika
Salt and black pepper to taste
1 tsp almond flour
1 tbsp butter
3/4 cup coconut cream

Directions and Total Time: approx. 30 minutes

Pat dry the pork pieces with a paper towel and season with paprika, salt, pepper, and sprinkle with almond flour. Melt butter in a skillet and sauté the pork until lightly browned, 5 minutes. Stir in cream; let boil. Cook until the sauce slightly thickens, 7 minutes. Serve over a bed of cauli rice.

Per serving: Cal 310; Net Carbs 2.5g; Fat 21g; Protein 26g

Mushroom & Pork Casserole

Ingredients for 4 servings

1 cup portobello mushrooms, chopped
1 cup ricotta, crumbled
1 cup Italian cheese blend
4 carrots, thinly sliced
Salt and black pepper to taste
1 clove garlic, minced
1 ¼ pounds ground pork
4 green onions, chopped
15 oz canned tomatoes
4 tbsp pork rinds, crushed
¼ cup chopped parsley
3 tbsp olive oil
⅓ cup water

Directions and Total Time: approx. 38 minutes

Mix parsley, ricotta cheese, and Italian cheese blend in a bowl; set aside. Heat olive oil in a skillet and cook pork for 3 minutes. Add garlic, half of the green onions, mushrooms, and 2 tbsp of pork rinds. Continue cooking for 3 minutes. Stir in tomatoes and water and cook for 3 minutes. Sprinkle a baking dish with 2 tbsp of pork rinds, top with half of the carrots and a season of salt, 2/3 of the pork mixture, and the cheese mixture. Repeat the layering process a second time to exhaust the ingredients. Cover the baking dish with foil and bake for 20 minutes at 370 F. Remove the foil and brown the top of the casserole with the broiler side of the oven for 2 minutes.

Per serving: Cal 672; Net Carbs 7.9g; Fat 56g; Protein 34.8g

Tangy Lemon Pork Steaks with Mushrooms

Ingredients for 4 servings

8 oz white button mushrooms, chopped
4 large, bone-in pork steaks
2 tsp lemon pepper seasoning
3 tbsp olive oil
3 tbsp butter
1 cup beef stock
6 garlic cloves, minced
2 tbsp chopped parsley
1 lemon, thinly sliced

Directions and Total Time: approx. 30 minutes

Pat the pork dry with a paper towel and season with salt and lemon pepper. Heat 2 tbsp each of olive oil and butter in a skillet over medium heat and cook the meat until brown, 10 minutes; set aside. Add the remaining oil and butter to the skillet, pour in half of the stock to deglaze the bottom of the pan, add garlic and mushrooms, and cook until softened, 5 minutes. Return the pork, add lemon slices, and cook until the liquid reduces by two-thirds. Garnish with parsley, and serve with steamed green beans.

Per serving: Cal 505; Net Carbs 3.2g; Fat 32g; Protein 46g

Celery Braised Pork Shanks in Wine Sauce

Ingredients for 4 servings

3 tbsp olive oil
3 lb pork shanks
3 celery stalks, chopped
5 garlic cloves, minced
1 ½ cups crushed tomatoes
½ cup red wine
¼ tsp red chili flakes
¼ cup chopped parsley

Directions and Total Time: approx. 2 hours 30 minutes

Preheat oven to 300 F. Heat olive oil in a Dutch oven and brown pork on all sides for 4 minutes; set aside. Add celery and garlic and sauté for 3 minutes. Return the pork and top with tomatoes, red wine, and chili flakes. Cover the lid and put the pot in the oven. Cook for 2 hours, turning the meat every 30 minutes. In the last 15 minutes, open the lid and increase the temperature to 450 F. Take out the pot, stir in parsley, and serve the meat with sauce on a bed of creamy mashed cauliflower.

Per serving: Cal 520; Net Carbs 1.4g; Fat 20g; Protein 75g

Tuscan Pork Tenderloin with Cauli Rice

Ingredients for 4 servings
1 cup loosely packed fresh baby spinach
2 tbsp olive oil
1 ½ lb pork tenderloin, cubed
Salt and black pepper to taste
½ tsp cumin powder
2 cups cauliflower rice
½ cup water
1 cup grape tomatoes, halved
3/4 cup crumbled feta cheese

Directions and Total Time: approx. 30 minutes
Heat olive oil in a skillet, season the pork with salt, pepper, and cumin, and sear on both sides for 5 minutes until brown. Stir in cauli rice and pour in water. Cook for 5 minutes or until cauliflower softens. Mix in spinach to wilt, 1 minute, and add the tomatoes. Spoon the dish into bowls, sprinkle with feta cheese, and serve with hot sauce.

Per serving: Cal 377; Net Carbs 1.9g; Fat 17g; Protein 43g

Indian Pork Masala

Ingredients for 4 servings
1 ½ lb pork shoulder, cut into bite-size pieces
2 tbsp ghee
1 tbsp freshly grated ginger
2 tbsp freshly pureed garlic
6 medium red onions, sliced
1 cup crushed tomatoes
2 tbsp Greek yogurt
½ tsp chili powder
2 tbsp garam masala
1 bunch cilantro, chopped
2 green chilies, sliced

Directions and Total Time: approx. 30 minutes
Bring a pot of water to a boil to blanch meat for 3 minutes; drain and set aside. Melt ghee in a skillet and sauté ginger, garlic, and onions until caramelized, 5 minutes. Mix in tomatoes, yogurt, and pork. Season with chili, garam masala, salt, and pepper. Stir and cook for 10 minutes. Stir in cilantro and green chilies. Serve masala with cauli rice.

Per serving: Cal 302; Net Carbs 2.2g; Fat 16g; Protein 33g

Cheesy Sausages in Creamy Onion Sauce

Ingredients for 4 servings

2 tsp almond flour
1 (16 oz) pork sausages
6 tbsp golden flaxseed meal
1 egg, beaten
1 tbsp olive oil
8 oz cream cheese, softened
3 tbsp freshly chopped chives
3 tsp freshly pureed onion
3 tbsp chicken broth
2 tbsp almond milk

Directions and Total Time: approx. 30 minutes

In a plate, mix flour with salt and pepper, and pour flaxseed meal to a plate. Prick the sausages with a fork all around, roll in the flour, in the egg, and then in the flaxseed meal. Heat olive oil in a skillet and fry sausages until brown, 15 minutes. Transfer to a plate and keep warm. In a saucepan, combine cream cheese, chives, onion, broth, and milk. Cook and stir over medium heat until smooth and evenly mixed, 5 minutes. Plate the sausages and spoon the sauce on top. Serve immediately with steamed broccoli.

Per serving: Cal 461; Net Carbs 0.5g; Fat 32g; Protein 34g

Savory Jalapeño Pork Meatballs

Ingredients for 4 servings

3 green onions, chopped
1 tbsp garlic powder
1 pound ground pork
1 jalapeño pepper, chopped
1 tsp dried oregano
2 tsp parsley
½ tsp Italian seasoning
2 tsp cumin
Salt and black pepper to taste
3 tbsp butter melted + 2 tbsp
4 ounces cream cheese
1 tsp turmeric
¼ tsp xylitol
½ tsp baking powder
1 ½ cups flax meal
½ cup almond flour

Directions and Total Time: approx. 45 minutes

Preheat oven to 350 F. In a food processor, add green onions, garlic powder, jalapeño pepper, and ½ cup water; blend well. Set a pan, warm in 2 tbsp of butter and cook ground pork for 3 minutes. Stir in onion mixture, and cook for 2 minutes. Stir in parsley, cloves, salt, cumin, ½ teaspoon turmeric, oregano, Italian seasoning, and pepper, and cook for 3 minutes. In a bowl, combine the remaining turmeric with almond flour, xylitol, flax meal, and baking powder. In a separate bowl, combine 3 tbsp melted butter with cream cheese. Combine the 2 mixtures to obtain a dough. Form balls from this mixture, set on a parchment paper, and roll each into a circle. Split the pork mixture on one-half of the dough circles, cover with the other half, seal edges, and lay on a lined sheet. Bake for 25 minutes.

Per serving: Cal 598; Net Carbs 5.3g; Fat 45.8g; Protein 35g

Greek-Style Pork Packets with Halloumi

Ingredients for 4 servings

1 lb turnips, cubed
½ cup salsa verde
2 tsp chili powder
1 tsp cumin powder
4 boneless pork chops
Salt and black pepper to taste
3 tbsp olive oil
4 slices halloumi cheese, cubed

Directions and Total Time: approx. 30 minutes

Preheat the grill to 400 F. Cut out four 18x12-inch sheets of heavy-duty aluminum foil. Grease the sheets with cooking spray. In a bowl, combine turnips, salsa verde, chili, and cumin. Season with salt and pepper. Place a pork chop on each foil sheet, spoon the turnip mixture on the meat, divide olive oil on top, and then halloumi cheese. Wrap the foil and place on the grill grate and cook for 10 minutes. Turn the foil packs over and cook further for 8 minutes. Remove the packs onto plates, and serve.

Per serving: Cal 501; Net Carbs 2.1g; Fat 27g; Protein 52g

Pork & Bacon Parcels

Ingredients for 4 servings

4 bacon strips
2 tbsp fresh parsley, chopped
4 pork loin chops, boneless
⅓ cup cottage cheese
1 tbsp olive oil
1 onion, chopped
1 tbsp garlic powder
2 tomatoes, chopped
⅓ cup chicken stock
Salt and black pepper, to taste

Directions and Total Time: approx. 40 minutes

Lay a bacon strip on top of each pork chop, then divide the parsley and cottage cheese on top. Roll each pork piece and secure with toothpicks. Set a pan over medium heat and warm oil, cook the pork parcels until browned, and remove to a plate. Add in the onion, and cook for 5 minutes. Pour in the chicken stock and garlic powder, and cook for 3 minutes. Get rid of the toothpicks from the rolls and return them to the pan. Stir in black pepper, salt, parsley, and tomatoes, bring to a boil, set heat to medium-low, and cook for 25 minutes while covered. Serve.

Per serving: Cal 433; Net Carbs 6.8g; Fat 23g; Protein 44.6g

Hot Pork Chops with Satay Sauce

Ingredients for 4 servings
2 lb boneless pork loin chops, cut into 2-inch pieces
Salt and black pepper to taste
1 medium white onion, sliced
1/3 cup peanut butter
¼ cup tamari sauce
½ tsp garlic powder
½ tsp onion powder
½ tsp hot sauce
1 cup chicken broth, divided
3 tbsp xanthan gum
1 tbsp chopped peanuts

Directions and Total Time: approx. 80 minutes
Season pork with salt and pepper; put into a pot and add onion. In a bowl, combine peanut butter, tamari sauce, garlic and onion powders, hot sauce, and two-thirds of the chicken broth. Pour the mixture over the meat. Bring to a boil over high heat, reduce the heat, and simmer for 1 hour or until the meat becomes tender. In a bowl, combine the remaining broth and xanthan gum. Stir the mixture into the meat and simmer until the sauce thickens, 2 minutes. Spoon onto a plate, garnish with peanuts and serve.
Per serving: Cal 455; Net Carbs 6.7g; Fat 17g; Protein 61g

Turnip Pork Pie

Ingredients for 8 servings
1 cup turnip mash
2 pounds ground pork
½ cup water
1 onion, chopped
1 tbsp sage
2 tbsp butter
Crust:
2 oz butter
1 egg
2 oz cheddar, shredded
2 cups almond flour
¼ tsp xanthan gum
A pinch of salt

Directions and Total Time: approx. 50 minutes
Stir all crust ingredients in a bowl. Make 2 balls out of the mixture and refrigerate for 10 minutes. In a pan, warm 2 tbsp of butter and sauté onion and ground pork for 8 minutes. Let cool for a few minutes and add in turnip mash and sage. Mix with hands. Roll out the pie crusts and place one at the bottom of a greased pie pan. Spread filling over the crust and top with the other coat. Bake in the oven for 30 minutes at 350 F. Serve.
Per serving: Cal 477; Net Carbs 1.7g; Fat 36.1g; Protein 33g

Sweet Pork Chops with Hoisin Sauce

Ingredients for 4 servings
4 oz hoisin sauce, sugar-free
1 ¼ pounds pork chops
Salt and black pepper to taste
1 tbsp xylitol
½ tsp ginger powder
2 tsp smoked paprika

Directions and Total Time: approx. 2 hours 20 minutes
In a bowl, mix pepper, xylitol, ginger, and paprika; rub pork chops with the mixture. Cover with plastic wraps and refrigerate for 2 hours. Preheat grill. Grill the meat for 2 minutes per side. Reduce the heat and brush with the hoisin sauce, cover, and grill for 5 minutes. Turn the meat and brush again with hoisin sauce. Cook for 5 minutes.
Per serving: Cal 352; Net Carbs 2.5g; Fat 22.9g; Protein 37g

Basil Pork Meatballs in Tomato Sauce

Ingredients for 6 servings
1 pound ground pork
2 green onions, chopped
1 tbsp olive oil
1 cup pork rinds, crushed
3 cloves garlic, minced
½ cup buttermilk
2 eggs, beaten
1 cup asiago cheese, shredded
Salt and black pepper to taste
1 can (29-ounce) tomato sauce
1 cup pecorino cheese, grated
Chopped basil to garnish

Directions and Total Time: approx. 45 minutes
Preheat oven to 370 F. Mix buttermilk, ground pork, garlic, asiago cheese, eggs, salt, pepper, and pork rinds in a bowl, until combined. Shape pork mixture into balls and place into a greased baking pan. Bake for 20 minutes. Remove and pour in tomato sauce and sprinkle with Pecorino cheese. Cover the pan with foil and put it back in the oven for 10 minutes. Remove the foil and cooking for 5 more minutes. Garnish with basil and serve.
Per serving: Cal 623; Net Carbs 4.6g; Fat 51.8g; Protein 53g

Canadian Pork Pie

Ingredients for 8 servings

1 cup cooked and mashed cauliflower
1 egg
¼ cup butter
2 cups almond flour
¼ tsp xanthan gum
¼ cup shredded mozzarella
2 pounds ground pork
⅓ cup pureed onion
¾ tsp allspice
1 tbsp ground sage
2 tbsp butter

Directions and Total Time: approx. 1 hour 40 minutes

Preheat oven to 350 F. Whisk egg, butter, almond flour, mozzarella cheese, and salt in a bowl. Make 2 balls out of the mixture and refrigerate for 10 minutes. Melt butter in a pan and cook ground pork, salt, onion, and allspice for 5-6 minutes. Remove to a bowl and mix in cauliflower and sage. Roll out the pie balls and place one at the bottom of a greased pie pan. Spread the pork mixture over the crust. Top with the other coat. Bake for 50 minutes then serve.

Per serving: Cal 485; Net Carbs 4g; Fat 41g; Protein 29g

Quick Pork Lo Mein

Ingredients for 4 servings

4 boneless pork chops, cut into ¼-inch strips
1 cup green beans, halved
1 cup shredded mozzarella
1 egg yolk
1-inch ginger knob, grated
3 tbsp sesame oil
Salt and black pepper to taste
1 red bell pepper, sliced
1 yellow bell pepper, sliced
1 garlic clove, minced
4 green onions, chopped
1 tsp toasted sesame seeds
3 tbsp coconut aminos
2 tsp sugar-free maple syrup
1 tsp fresh ginger paste

Directions and Total Time: approx. 25 min + chilling time

Microwave mozzarella cheese for 2 minutes. Let cool for 1 minute and mix in the egg yolk until well-combined. Lay a parchment paper on a flat surface, pour the cheese mixture on top and cover with another parchment paper. Flatten the dough into 1/8-inch thickness. Take off the parchment paper and cut the dough into thin spaghetti strands. Place in a bowl and refrigerate overnight. Bring 2 cups water to a boil in saucepan and add in pasta. Cook for 1 minute and drain; set aside. Heat sesame oil in a skillet, season pork with salt and pepper, and sear on both sides for 5 minutes. Transfer to a plate. In the same skillet, mix in bell peppers, green beans and cook for 3 minutes. Stir in garlic, ginger, and green onions and cook for 1 minute. Add pork and pasta to the skillet and toss well. In a bowl, toss coconut aminos, remaining sesame oil, maple syrup, and ginger paste. Pour the mixture over the pork mixture; cook for 1 minute. Garnish with sesame seeds to serve.

Per serving: Cal 338; Fats 12g; Net Carbs 4.6g; Protein 43g

Tasty Sambal Pork Noodles

Ingredients for 4 servings

2 (8 oz) packs Miracle noodles, garlic, and herb
1 tbsp olive oil
1 lb ground pork
4 garlic cloves, minced
1-inch ginger, grated
1 tsp liquid stevia
1 tbsp tomato paste
2 fresh basil leaves, chopped
2 tbsp sambal oelek
2 tbsp plain vinegar
2 tbsp coconut aminos
Salt to taste
1 tbsp unsalted butter

Directions and Total Time: approx. 60 minutes

Bring 2 cups water to a boil Strain the Miracle noodles and rinse well under hot running water. Allow proper draining and pour them into the boiling water. Cook for 3 minutes and strain again. Place a dry skillet and stir-fry the shirataki noodles until visibly dry, 1-2 minutes. Season with salt and set aside. Heat olive oil in a pot and cook for 5 minutes. Stir in garlic, ginger, and stevia and cook for 1 minute. Add in tomato paste and mix in sambal oelek, vinegar, 1 cup water, aminos, and salt. Continue cooking over low heat for 30 minutes. Add in shirataki, butter; mix well into the sauce. Garnish with basil and serve.

Per serving: Cal 505; Fats 30g; Net Carbs 8.2g; Protein 34g

Pasta & Cheese Pulled Pork

Ingredients for 4 servings

1 cup shredded mozzarella cheese1
lb pork shoulders, divided into 3 pieces
1 egg yolk
2 tbsp olive oil
Salt and black pepper to taste
1 tsp dried thyme
1 cup chicken broth
2 tbsp butter
2 medium shallots, minced
2 garlic cloves, minced
1 cup grated Monterey Jack
4 oz cream cheese, softened
1 cup heavy cream
½ tsp white pepper
½ tsp nutmeg powder
2 tbsp chopped parsley

Directions and Total Time: approx. 100 min + chilling time

Microwave mozzarella cheese for 2 minutes. Take out the bowl and allow cooling for 1 minute. Mix in egg yolk until well-combined. Lay a parchment paper on a flat surface, pour the cheese mixture on top and cover with another parchment paper. Flatten the dough into 1/8-inch thickness. Take off the parchment paper and cut the dough into small cubes of the size of macaroni. Place in a bowl and refrigerate overnight. Bring 2 cups water to a boil and add in keto macaroni. Cook for 1 minute and drain; set aside. Heat olive oil in a pot, season pork with salt, pepper, and thyme and sear on both sides until brown. Pour in broth, cover, and cook over low heat for 1 hour or until softened. Remove to a plate and shred into small strands. Set aside. Preheat oven to 380 F. Melt butter in a skillet and sauté shallots and garlic for 3 minutes. Pour in 1 cup water to deglaze the pot and stir in half of Monterey Jack and cream cheeses for 4 minutes. Mix in heavy cream and season with salt, pepper, white pepper, and nutmeg powder. Mix in pasta and pork. Pour mixture into a baking dish and cover with remaining Monterey Jack cheese. Bake for 20 minutes. Garnish with parsley and serve.

Per serving: Cal 603; Fats 43g; Net Carbs 4.5g; Protein 46g

Baked Tenderloin with Lime Chimichurri

Ingredients for 4 servings

1 lime, juiced
¼ cup chopped mint leaves
¼ cup rosemary, chopped
2 cloves garlic, minced
¼ cup olive oil
4 lb pork tenderloin
Salt and black pepper to taste
Olive oil for rubbing

Directions and Total Time: approx. 1 hour 10 minutes

In a bowl, mix mint, rosemary, garlic, lime juice, olive oil, and salt, and combine well; set aside. Preheat charcoal grill to 450 F creating a direct heat area and indirect heat area. Rub the pork with olive oil, season with salt and pepper. Place the meat over direct heat and sear for 3 minutes on each side; then move to the indirect heat area. Close the lid and cook for 25 minutes on one side, then open, flip, and grill closed for 20 minutes. Remove from the grill and let sit for 5 minutes before slicing. Spoon lemon chimichurri over the pork and serve.

Per serving: Cal 388, Net Carbs 2.1g, Fat 18g, Protein 28g

Green Bean Creamy Pork with Fettuccine

Ingredients for 4 servings

4 pork loin medallions, cut into thin strips
1 cup shredded mozzarella
1 cup shaved Parmesan cheese
1 egg yolk
1 tbsp olive oil
Salt and black pepper to taste
½ cup green beans, chopped
1 lemon, zested and juiced
¼ cup chicken broth
1 cup crème fraiche
6 basil leaves, chopped

Directions and Total Time: approx. 40 min + chilling time

Microwave mozzarella cheese for 2 minutes. Allow cooling for 1 minute. Mix in egg yolk until well-combined. Lay a parchment paper on a flat surface, pour the cheese mixture on top and cover with another parchment paper. Flatten the dough into 1/8-inch thickness. Take off the parchment paper and cut the dough into thick fettuccine strands. Place in a bowl and refrigerate overnight. Bring 2 cups water to a boil in saucepan and add the fettuccine. Cook for 1 minute and drain; set aside. Heat olive oil in a skillet, season the pork with salt and pepper, and cook for 10 minutes. Mix in green beans and cook for 5 minutes. Stir in lemon zest, lemon juice, and chicken broth. Cook for 5 more minutes. Add crème fraiche, fettuccine, and basil and cook for 1 minute. Top with Parmesan cheese.

Per serving: Cal 586; Fats 32.3g; Net Carbs 9g; Protein 59g

Cauliflower Pork Goulash

Ingredients for 4 servings
2 tbsp butter
1 cup mushrooms, sliced
1 ½ pounds ground pork
Salt and black pepper, to taste
2 cups cauliflower florets
1 onion, chopped
14 ounces canned tomatoes
1 garlic clove, minced
1 tbsp smoked paprika
2 tbsp parsley, chopped
1 tbsp tomato puree
1 ½ cups water

Directions and Total Time: approx. 30 minutes
Melt butter in a pan over medium heat, stir in pork, and brown for 5 minutes. Place in mushrooms, garlic, and onion, and cook for 4 minutes. Stir in paprika, water, tomatoes, tomato paste, and cauliflower, bring to a simmer and cook for 20 minutes. Add in pepper, salt and parsley.

Per serving: Cal 533; Net Carbs 7g; Fat 41.8g; Protein 35.5g

Basil Prosciutto Pizza

Ingredients for 4 servings
4 prosciutto slices, cut into thirds
2 cups grated mozzarella cheese
2 tbsp cream cheese, softened
½ cup almond flour
1 egg, beaten
⅓ cup tomato sauce
⅓ cup sliced mozzarella
6 fresh basil leaves, to serve

Directions and Total Time: approx. 45 minutes
Preheat oven to 390 F and line a pizza pan with parchment paper. Microwave mozzarella cheese and 2 tbsp of cream cheese for 1 minute. Mix in almond meal and egg.
Spread the mixture on the pizza pan and bake for 15 minutes; set aside. Spread the tomato sauce on the crust. Arrange the mozzarella slices on the sauce and then the prosciutto. Bake again for 15 minutes or until the cheese melts. Remove and top with the basil. Slice and serve.

Per serving: Cal 160; Net Carbs 0.5g; Fats 6.2g; Protein 22g

Bell Pepper Noodles with Pork Avocado

Ingredients for 4 servings

2 lb red and yellow bell peppers, spiralized
2 tbsp butter
1 lb ground pork
Salt and black pepper to taste
1 tsp garlic powder
2 avocados, pitted, mashed
2 tbsp chopped pecans

Directions and Total Time: approx. 15 minutes

Melt butter in a skillet and cook the pork until brown, 5 minutes. Season with salt and pepper. Stir in bell peppers, garlic powder and cook until the peppers are slightly tender, 2 minutes. Mix in mashed avocados and cook for 1 minute. Garnish with the pecans and serve warm.

Per serving: Cal 704; Fats 49g; Net Carbs 9.3g; Protein 35g

Caribbean Jerk Pork

Ingredients for 4 servings

1 ½ pounds pork roast
1 tbsp olive oil
¼ cup jerk seasoning
2 tbsp soy sauce, sugar-free
½ cup vegetable stock

Directions and Total Time: approx. 4 hours 20 minutes

Preheat oven to 350 F and rub the pork with olive oil and jerk seasoning. Heat olive oil in a pan over medium heat and sear the meat well on all sides, about 4-5 minutes. Put the pork in a baking dish, add in the vegetable stock and soy sauce, cover with aluminium foil and bake for 45 minutes, turning once halfway. Then, remove the foil and continue cooking until completely cooked through. Serve.

Per serving: Cal 407; Net Carbs 5.6g; Fat 20g; Protein 46g

Parmesan Pork with Green Pasta

Ingredients for 4 servings
4 boneless pork chops
Salt and black pepper to taste
½ cup basil pesto
1 cup grated Parmesan cheese
1 tbsp butter
4 large turnips, spiralized

Directions and Total Time: approx. 1 hour 30 minutes
Preheat oven to 350 F. Season pork with salt and pepper and place on a greased baking sheet. Spread pesto on the pork and bake for 45 minutes. Pull out the baking sheet and divide half of Parmesan cheese on top of the pork. Cook further for 5 minutes; set aside. Melt butter in a skillet and sauté the turnips for 7 minutes. Stir in the remaining Parmesan and serve in plates, topped with the pork.
Per serving: Cal 532; Fats 28g; Net Carbs 4.9g; Protein 54g

Grilled BBQ Pork Chops

Ingredients for 4 servings
4 pork loin chops, boneless
½ cup sugar-free BBQ sauce
1 tbsp erythritol
½ tsp ginger powder
½ tsp garlic powder
2 tsp smoked paprika

Directions and Total Time: approx. 1 hour 50 minutes
In a bowl, mix black pepper, erythritol, ginger powder, ½ tsp garlic powder, and smoked paprika, and rub pork chops on all sides with the mixture. Cover the pork chops with plastic wraps and place in the refrigerator for 90 minutes. Preheat grill. Unwrap the meat, place on the grill grate, and cook for 2 minutes per side. Reduce the heat and brush with BBQ sauce; grill for 5 minutes. Flip and brush again with BBQ sauce. Cook for 5 minutes. Serve.
Per serving: Cal 363, Net Carbs 0g, Fat 26.6g, Protein 34.1g

Pecorino Romano Kohlrabi with Sausage

Ingredients for 4 servings

1 cup grated Pecorino Romano cheese

2 tbsp olive oil

1 cup sliced pork sausage

4 bacon slices, chopped

4 large kohlrabi, spiralized

6 garlic cloves, minced

1 cup cherry tomatoes, halved

7 fresh basil leaves

1 tbsp pine nuts for topping

Directions and Total Time: approx. 15 minutes

Heat olive oil in a skillet and cook sausage and bacon until brown, 5 minutes. Transfer to a plate. Stir in kohlrabi and garlic and cook until tender, 5-7 minutes. Add in cherry tomatoes, salt, and pepper and cook for 2 minutes. Mix in the sausage, bacon, basil, and Pecorino Romano cheese. Garnish with pine nuts and serve warm.

Per serving: Cal 229; Fats 20.2g; Net Carbs 2.4g; Protein 8g

Swiss Pork Patties with Salad

Ingredients for 4 servings

1 lb ground pork

3 tbsp olive oil

2 hearts romaine lettuce, torn

2 firm tomatoes, sliced

¼ red onion, sliced

3 oz Swiss cheese, shredded

Directions and Total Time: approx. 30 minutes

Season pork with salt and pepper, mix, and shape several medium-sized patties. Heat 2 tbsp oil in a skillet and fry the patties on both sides for 10 minutes. Transfer to a wire rack to drain oil. When cooled, cut into quarters. Mix lettuce, tomatoes, and onion in a bowl, season with oil, salt and pepper. Toss and add the patties on top. Microwave the cheese for 90 seconds, drizzle it over the salad.

Per serving: Cal 310, Net Carbs 2g, Fat 23g, Protein 22g

Maple Scallion Pork Bites

Ingredients for 4 servings
½ cup + 1 tbsp red wine
1 tbsp + 1/3 cup tamari sauce
1 pork tenderloin, cubed
½ cup sugar-free maple syrup
½ cup sesame seeds
1 tbsp sesame oil
1 tsp freshly pureed garlic
½ tsp freshly grated ginger
1 scallion, finely chopped

Directions and Total Time: approx. 50 minutes
Preheat oven to 350 F. In a zipper bag, combine ½ cup of red wine with 1 tbsp of tamari sauce. Add in pork cubes, seal the bag, and marinate the meat in the fridge overnight. Remove from the fridge and drain. Pour maple syrup and sesame seeds into two separate bowls; roll the pork in maple syrup and then in the sesame seeds. Place on a greased baking sheet and bake for 35 minutes. In a bowl, mix the remaining wine, tamari sauce, sesame oil, garlic, and ginger. Pour the sauce into a bowl. Transfer pork to a platter and garnish with scallions. Serve with sauce.
Per serving: Cal 352; Net Carbs 6.4g; Fat 18g; Protein 39g

Pork Medallions with Pancetta

Ingredients for 4 servings
1 lb pork loin, cut into medallions
2 onions, chopped
6 pancetta slices, chopped
½ cup vegetable stock
Salt and black pepper, to taste

Directions and Total Time: approx. 55 minutes
Set a pan over medium heat, and cook the pancetta until crispy; remove to a plate. Add onions and stir-fry for 5 minutes; set aside to the same plate as pancetta. Add pork medallions to the pan, season with pepper and salt, brown for 3 minutes on each side, turn, reduce heat, and cook for 7 minutes. Stir in the stock, and cook for 2 minutes. Return the pancetta and onions and cook for 1 minute.
Per serving: Cal 325, Net Carbs 6g, Fat 18g, Protein 36g

Golden Pork Chops with Mushrooms

Ingredients for 6 servings
2 (14-oz) cans Mushroom soup
1 onion, chopped
6 pork chops
½ cup sliced mushrooms
Salt and black pepper to taste

Directions and Total Time: approx. 1 hour 15 minutes
Preheat the oven to 375 F. Season the pork chops with salt and pepper, and place them in a baking dish. Combine the soup, mushrooms, and onions in a bowl. Pour this mixture over the pork chops. Bake for 45 minutes.

Per serving: Cal 403; Net Carbs 8g; Fat 32.6g; Protein 19g

Cumin Pork Chops

Ingredients for 4 servings
4 pork chops
¾ cup cumin powder
1 tsp chili powder
Salt and black pepper to taste

Directions and Total Time: approx. 25 minutes
In a bowl, combine the cumin with black pepper, salt, and chili. Place in the pork chops and rub them well. Heat a grill over medium temperature, add in the pork chops, cook for 5 minutes, flip, and cook for 5 minutes.

Per serving: Cal 349; Net Carbs 4g; Fat 18.6g; Protein 42g

SEAFOOD

Spicy Smoked Mackerel Cakes

Ingredients for 6 servings

4 smoked mackerel steaks, bones removed, flaked
1 rutabaga, peeled and diced
Salt and chili pepper to taste
3 tbsp olive oil + for rubbing
3 eggs, beaten
2 tbsp mayonnaise
1 tbsp pork rinds, crushed

Directions and Total Time: approx. 30 minutes

Bring rutabaga to boil in salted water for 8 minutes. Drain, transfer to a mixing bowl, and mash the lumps. Add mackerel, eggs, mayonnaise, pork rinds, salt, and chili pepper. Make 6 compact patties. Heat olive oil in a skillet and fry the patties for 3 minutes on each side. Remove onto a wire rack to cool. Serve cakes with sesame sauce.

Per serving: Cal 324; Net Carbs 2.2g; Fat 27g; Protein 16g

Stuffed Avocado with Yogurt & Crabmeat

Ingredients for 4 servings

3 oz plain yogurt, strained overnight in a cheesecloth
1 tsp olive oil
1 cup crabmeat
2 avocados, halved and pitted
¼ cup almonds, chopped
1 tsp smoked paprika
Salt and black pepper, to taste

Directions and Total Time: approx. 25 minutes

Set oven to 425 F. Grease oil on a baking pan. In a bowl, mix crabmeat, yogurt, salt, and pepper. Fill avocado halves with almonds and crabmeat/cheese mixture and bake for 18 minutes. Decorate with paprika to serve.

Per serving: Cal 264; Net Carbs 11g; Fat 24.4g; Protein 4g

Hazelnut Cod Fillets

Ingredients for 2 servings

2 cod fillets
2 tbsp ghee
¼ cup roasted hazelnuts
A pinch of cayenne pepper

Directions and Total Time: approx. 30 minutes

Preheat your oven to 425 F. Line a baking dish with waxed paper. Melt the ghee and brush it over the fish. In a food processor, combine the rest of the ingredients. Coat the cod with the hazelnut mixture. Place in the oven and bake for about 15 minutes. Serve.

Per serving: Cal 467; Net Carbs 2.8g; Fat 31g; Protein 40g

Wine Shrimp Scampi Pizza

Ingredients for 4 servings

½ cup almond flour
¼ tsp salt
2 tbsp ground psyllium husk
3 tbsp olive oil
2 tbsp butter
2 garlic cloves, minced
¼ cup white wine
½ tsp dried basil
½ tsp dried parsley
½ lemon, juiced
½ lb shrimp, deveined
2 cups grated cheese blend
½ tsp Italian seasoning
¼ cup grated Parmesan

Directions and Total Time: approx. 35 minutes

Preheat oven to 390 F and line a baking sheet with parchment paper. In a bowl, mix almond flour, salt, psyllium powder, 1 tbsp of olive oil, and 1 cup of lukewarm water until dough forms. Spread the mixture on the pizza pan and bake for 10 minutes. Heat butter and the remaining olive oil in a skillet. Sauté garlic for 30 seconds. Mix in white wine, reduce by half, and stir in basil, parsley and lemon juice. Stir in shrimp and cook for 3 minutes. Mix in the cheese blend and Italian seasoning. Let the cheese melt, 3 minutes. Spread the shrimp mixture on the crust and top with Parmesan cheese. Bake for 5 minutes or until Parmesan melts. Slice and serve warm.

Per serving: Cal 423; Net Carbs 3.9g; Fats 34g; Protein 23g

Shallot Mussel with Shirataki

Ingredients for 4 servings
2 (8 oz) packs angel hair shirataki
1 lb mussels
1 cup white wine
4 tbsp olive oil
3 shallots, finely chopped
6 garlic cloves, minced
2 tsp red chili flakes
½ cup fish stock
1 ½ cups heavy cream
2 tbsp chopped fresh parsley
Salt and black pepper to taste

Directions and Total Time: approx. 25 minutes
Bring 2 cups of water to a boil in a pot. Strain the shirataki pasta and rinse well under hot running water. Drain and transfer to the boiling water. Cook for 3 minutes and strain again. Place a large dry skillet and stir-fry the shirataki pasta until visibly dry, 1-2 minutes; set aside. Pour mussels and white wine into a pot, cover, and cook for 3-4 minutes. Strain mussels and reserve the cooking liquid. Let cool, discard any closed mussels, and remove the meat out of ¾ of the mussel shells. Set aside with the remaining mussels in the shells. Heat olive oil in a skillet and sauté shallots, garlic, and chili flakes for 3 minutes. Mix in reduced wine and fish stock. Allow boiling and whisk in remaining butter and then the heavy cream. Season with salt, and pepper, and mix in parsley. Pour in shirataki pasta, mussels and toss well in the sauce. Serve.
Per serving: Cal 471; Net Carbs 6.9g; Fats 34g; Protein 18g

Nori Shrimp Rolls

Ingredients for 5 servings
2 cups cooked shrimp
1 tbsp Sriracha sauce
¼ cucumber, julienned
5 hand roll nori sheets
¼ cup mayonnaise
1 tbsp dill

Directions and Total Time: approx. 10 minutes
Chop the shrimp and combine with mayo, dill, and sriracha sauce in a bowl. Place a single nori sheet on a flat surface and spread about a fifth of the shrimp mixture. Roll the nori sheet as desired. Repeat with the other ingredients.
Per serving: Cal 130; Net Carbs 1g; Fat 10g; Protein 8.7g

Hazelnut-Crusted Salmon

Ingredients for 4 servings
4 salmon fillets
Salt and black pepper to taste
¼ cup mayonnaise
½ cup chopped hazelnuts
1 chopped shallot
2 tsp lemon zest
1 tbsp olive oil
1 cup heavy cream

Directions and Total Time: approx. 35 minutes
Preheat oven to 360 F. Brush the salmon with mayonnaise and coat with hazelnuts. Place in a lined baking dish and bake for 15 minutes. Heat olive oil in a saucepan and sauté shallot for 3 minutes. Stir in lemon zest and heavy cream and bring to a boil; cook until thickened, 5 minutes. Adjust seasoning and drizzle the sauce over the fish to serve.

Per serving: Cal 563; Net Carbs 6g; Fat 47g; Protein 34g

Fish & Cauliflower Parmesan Gratin

Ingredients for 4 servings
1 head cauliflower, cut into florets
2 cod fillets, cubed
3 white fish fillets, cubed
1 tbsp butter, melted
1 cup crème fraiche
¼ cup grated Parmesan
Grated Parmesan for topping

Directions and Total Time: approx. 40 minutes
Preheat oven to 400 F. Coat fish cubes and broccoli with butter. Spread in a greased baking dish. Mix crème fraiche with Parmesan cheese, pour and smear the cream on the fish, and sprinkle with some more Parmesan cheese. Bake for 25-30 minutes. Let sit for 5 minutes and serve in plates.

Per serving: Cal 354; Net Carbs 4g; Fat 17g; Protein 28g

Broccoli & Fish Gratin

Ingredients for 4 servings

¼ cup grated Pecorino Romano cheese + some more
2 salmon fillets, cubed
3 white fish, cubed
1 broccoli, cut into florets
1 tbsp butter, melted
Salt and black pepper to taste
1 cup crème fraiche

Directions and Total Time: approx. 45 minutes

Preheat oven to 400 F. Toss the fish cubes and broccoli in butter and season with salt and pepper. Spread in a greased dish. Mix crème fraiche with Pecorino Romano cheese, pour and smear the cream on the fish. Bake for 30 minutes. Serve with lemon-mustard asparagus.

Per serving: Cal 354; Net Carbs 4g; Fat 17g; Protein 28g

Salmon Caesar Salad with Poached Eggs

Ingredients for 4 servings

½ cup chopped smoked salmon
2 tbsp heinz low carb caesar dressing
3 cups water
8 eggs
2 cups torn romaine lettuce
6 slices pancetta

Directions and Total Time: approx. 15 minutes

Boil water in a pot for 5 minutes. Crack each egg into a small bowl and gently slide into the water. Poach for 2-3 minutes, remove, and transfer to a paper towel to dry. Poach the remaining 7 eggs. Put the pancetta in a skillet and fry for 6 minutes, turning once. Allow cooling, and chop into small pieces. Toss the lettuce, smoked salmon, pancetta, and caesar dressing in a salad bowl. Top with two eggs each, and serve immediately.

Per serving: Cal 260; Net Carbs 5g; Fat 21g; Protein 8g

Avocado & Cauliflower Salad with Prawns

Ingredients for 6 servings

1 cauliflower head, florets only
1 lb medium-sized prawns
¼ cup + 1 tbsp olive oil
1 avocado, chopped
3 tbsp chopped dill
¼ cup lemon juice
2 tbsp lemon zest

Directions and Total Time: approx. 30 minutes

Heat 1 tbsp olive oil in a skillet and cook the prawns for 8-10 minutes. Microwave cauliflower for 5 minutes. Place prawns, cauliflower, and avocado in a large bowl. Whisk together the remaining olive oil, lemon zest, juice, dill, and some salt and pepper, in another bowl. Pour the dressing over, toss to combine and serve immediately.

Per serving: Cal 214; Net Carbs 5g; Fat 17g; Protein 15g

Fish Fritters

Ingredients for 4 servings

1 pound cod fillets, sliced
¼ cup mayonnaise
¼ cup almond flour
2 eggs
Salt and black pepper to taste
1 cup Swiss cheese, grated
1 tbsp chopped dill
3 tbsp olive oil

Directions and Total Time: approx. 40 min + cooling time

Mix the fish, mayo, flour, eggs, salt, pepper, Swiss cheese, and dill, in a bowl. Cover the bowl with plastic wrap and refrigerate for 2 hours. Warm olive oil and fetch 2 tbsp of fish mixture into the skillet, use the back of a spatula to flatten the top. Cook for 4 minutes, flip, and fry for 4 more. Remove onto a wire rack and repeat until the fish batter is over; add more oil if needed.

Per serving: Cal 633; Net Carbs 7g; Fat 46.9g; Protein 39g

VEGAN & VEGETARIAN

Keto Brownies

Ingredients for 4 servings
2 tbsp flax seed powder
¼ cup cocoa powder
½ cup almond flour
½ tsp baking powder
½ cup erythritol
10 tbsp vegan butter
2 oz dairy-free dark chocolate
½ tsp vanilla extract

Directions and Total Time: approx. 30 min+ chilling time
Preheat oven to 375 F and line a baking sheet with parchment paper. Mix the flax seed powder with 6 tbsp water in a bowl and allow thickening for 5 minutes. In a separate bowl, mix cocoa powder, almond flour, baking powder, and erythritol until no lumps from the erythritol remain. In another bowl, add butter and dark chocolate and microwave both for 30 seconds. Whisk flax egg and vanilla into the chocolate mixture, then pour the mixture into the dry ingredients; mix well. Pour the batter onto the paper-lined sheet and bake for 20 minutes. Let cool completely and refrigerate for 2 hours. Slice into squares.
Per serving: Cal 227; Net Carbs 3g; Fat 19g; Protein 4g

Mixed Berry Yogurt Ice Pops

Ingredients for 6 servings
2/3 cup frozen strawberries & blueberries, thawed
2/3 cup avocado, halved, pitted
1 cup dairy-free yogurt
½ cup coconut cream
1 tsp vanilla extract

Directions and Total Time: approx. 2 min+ chilling time
Pour avocado pulp, berries, dairy-free yogurt, coconut cream, and vanilla extract. Process until smooth. Pour into ice pop sleeves and freeze for 8 hours. Serve when ready.
Per serving: Cal 80; Net Carbs 4g; Fat 5g; Protein 2g

Speedy Custard Tart

Ingredients for 4 servings

¼ cup butter, cold and crumbled
¼ cup almond flour
3 tbsp coconut flour
½ tsp salt
3 tbsp erythritol
1 ½ tsp vanilla extract
4 whole eggs
2 whole eggs + 3 egg yolks
½ cup swerve sugar
1 tsp vanilla bean paste
2 tbsp coconut flour
1 ¼ cup almond milk
1 ¼ cup heavy cream
2 tbsp sugar-free maple syrup
¼ cup chopped almonds

Directions and Total Time: approx. 75 minutes

Preheat oven to 350 F and grease a pie pan with cooking spray. In a bowl, mix almond flour, coconut flour, and salt. Add in butter and mix with an electric mixer until crumbly. Add in erythritol and vanilla extract and mix. Pour in the four eggs one after another while mixing until formed into a ball. Dust a clean flat surface with almond flour, unwrap the dough, and roll out the dough into a large rectangle, fit into the pie pan; prick the base of the crust. Bake until golden. Remove after and allow cooling.

In a mixing bowl, whisk the 2 whole eggs, 3 egg yolks, swerve sugar, vanilla bean paste, and coconut flour. Put almond milk, heavy cream, and maple syrup into a pot and bring to a boil. Pour the mixture into the egg mix and whisk while pouring. Run batter through a fine strainer into a bowl and skim off any froth. Remove the parchment paper, and transfer the egg batter into the pie. Bake for 45 minutes. Garnish with almonds, slice, and serve.

Per serving: Cal 459; Net Carbs 1.2g, Fat 40g, Protein 12g

Vegan Cheesecake with Blueberries

Ingredients for 6 servings

2 oz vegan butter
1 ¼ cups almond flour
3 tbsp Swerve sugar
½ tsp vanilla extract
3 tbsp flax seed powder
2 cups dairy-free cream cheese
½ cup coconut cream
1 tsp lemon zest
½ tsp vanilla extract
2 oz fresh blueberries

Directions and Total Time: approx. 70 min+ chilling time

Preheat oven to 350 F. Line a springform pan with parchment paper. Melt vegan butter in a skillet until nutty in flavor. Turn the heat off and stir in almond flour, 2 tbsp swerve, and vanilla until a dough forms. Press the mixture into the springform pan and bake for 8 minutes. Mix the flax seed powder with 9 tbsp water and allow sitting for 5 minutes. In a bowl, combine cream cheese, coconut cream, remaining swerve, lemon zest, vanilla extract, and flax egg. Remove the crust from oven and pour the mixture on top. Bake the cake for 15 minutes at 400 F. Reduce the heat 230 F and bake further for 50 minutes. Refrigerate overnight and scatter the blueberries on top.

Per serving: Cal 330; Net Carbs 4g; Fat 31g; Protein 8g

Pistachio Heart Biscuits

Ingredients for 4 servings

1 cup butter, softened
2/3 cup swerve sugar
1 large egg, beaten
2 tsp pistachio extract
2 cups almond flour
½ cup dark chocolate
Chopped pistachios

Directions and Total Time: approx. 30 min + cooling time

Add butter and swerve to a bowl; beat until smooth and creamy. Whisk in egg until combined. Mix in pistachio extract and flour until a smooth dough forms. Wrap the dough in plastic wrap and chill for 10 minutes. Preheat oven to 350 F and lightly dust a chopping board with some almond flour. Unwrap the dough and roll out to 2-inch thickness. Cut out as many biscuits as you can get while rerolling the trimming and making more biscuits. Arrange the biscuits on the parchment paper-lined baking sheet and bake for 15 minutes. Transfer to a wire rack to cool completely. In 2 separate bowls, melt chocolate in a microwave while adding some maple syrup for taste. Dip one side of each biscuit in the dark chocolate and then in the white chocolate. Garnish dark chocolate's side with the pistachios and cool on the wire rack.

Per serving: Cal 470; Net Carbs 3.4g, Fat 45g, Protein 6.2g

Lime Avocado Ice Cream

Ingredients for 4 servings
2 large avocados, pitted
Juice and zest of 3 limes
1/3 cup erythritol
1¾ cups coconut cream
¼ tsp vanilla extract

Directions and Total Time: approx. 10 minutes
In a blender, combine avocado pulp, lime juice and zest, erythritol, coconut cream, and vanilla extract. Process until smooth. Pour the mixture into an ice cream maker and freeze. When ready, remove and scoop the ice cream into bowls. Serve immediately.
Per serving: Cal 260; Net Carbs 4g; Fat 25g; Protein 4g

Blackberry Lemon Tarte Tatin

Ingredients for 4 servings
¼ cup butter, cold and crumbled
¼ cup almond flour
3 tbsp coconut flour
½ tsp salt
3 tbsp erythritol
1 ½ tsp vanilla extract
4 whole eggs
4 tbsp melted butter
3 tsp swerve brown sugar
1 cup fresh blackberries
1 tsp vanilla extract
1 lemon, juiced
1 cup ricotta cheese
4 fresh basil leaves to garnish
1 egg, lightly beaten

Directions and Total Time: approx. 50 minutes
Preheat oven to 350 F. In a bowl, mix almond and coconut flour, and salt. Add in butter and mix until crumbly. Mix in erythritol and vanilla extract. Pour in the 4 eggs and mix until formed into a ball. Flatten the dough on a clean flat surface, cover in plastic wrap, and refrigerate for 1 hour. Dust a clean flat surface with almond flour, unwrap the dough, and roll out the dough into a circle. In a greased baking pan, mix butter, swerve brown sugar, blackberries, vanilla extract, and lemon juice. Arrange blackberries uniformly across the pan. Lay the pastry over the fruit filling and tuck the sides into the pan. Brush with beaten egg and bake for 40 minutes. Turn the pie onto a plate, crumble ricotta cheese on top, and garnish with basil.
Per serving: Cal 465; Net Carbs 5.8g, Fat 41g, Protein 16g

SNACKS & SIDE DISHES

Delicious Pancetta Strawberries

Ingredients for 4 servings

2 tbsp swerve confectioner's sugar

1 cup mascarpone cheese

1/8 tsp white pepper

12 fresh strawberries

12 thin slices pancetta

Directions and Total Time: approx. 30 minutes

In a bowl, combine mascarpone, swerve, and white pepper. Coat strawberries in the cheese mixture, wrap each strawberry in a pancetta slice, and place on an ungreased baking sheet. Bake in the oven for 425 F for 15-20 minutes until pancetta browns and is crispy. Serve warm.

Per serving: Cal 171; Net Carbs 1.2g; Fat 11g; Protein 12g

Salami & Cheddar Skewers

Ingredients for 4 servings

¼ cup olive oil

1 tbsp plain vinegar

2 garlic cloves, minced

1 tsp dried Italian herb blend

4 oz hard salami, cubed

¼ cup pitted Kalamata olives

12 oz cheddar cheese, cubed

1 tsp chopped parsley

Directions and Total Time: approx. 4 hours

In a bowl, mix olive oil, vinegar, garlic, and herb blend. Add in salami, olives, and cheddar cheese. Mix until well coated. Cover the bowl with plastic wrap and marinate in the refrigerator for 4 hours. Remove, drain the marinade and skewer one salami cube, one olive, and one cheese cube. Repeat making more skewers with the remaining ingredients. Plate and garnish with the parsley to serve.

Per serving: Cal 585; Net Carbs 1.8g; Fat 52g; Protein 27g

Chives & Green Beans Ham Rolls

Ingredients for 4 servings
8 oz Havarti cheese, cut into 16 strips
16 thin slices deli ham, cut in half lengthwise
1 medium sweet red pepper, cut into 16 strips
1 ½ cups water
16 fresh green beans
2 tbsp salted butter
16 whole chives

Directions and Total Time: approx. 50 minutes
Bring the water to a boil in a skillet over medium heat. Add in green beans, cover, and cook for 3 minutes or until softened; drain. Melt butter in a skillet and sauté green beans for 2 minutes; transfer to a plate. Assemble 1 green bean, 1 strip of red pepper, 1 cheese strip, and wrap with a ham slice. Tie with one chive. Repeat the assembling process with the remaining ingredients and refrigerate.

Per serving: Cal 399; Net Carbs 8.7g; Fat 24g; Protein 35g

Savory Pan-Fried Cauliflower & Bacon

Ingredients for 4 servings
1 large head cauliflower, cut into florets
10 oz bacon, chopped
1 garlic clove, minced
Salt and black pepper to taste
2 tbsp parsley, finely chopped

Directions and Total Time: approx. 15 minutes
Pour cauliflower in salted boiling water over medium heat and cook for 5 minutes or until soft; drain and set aside. In a skillet, fry bacon until brown and crispy. Add cauliflower and garlic. Sauté until the cauli browns slightly. Season with salt and pepper. Garnish with parsley and serve.

Per serving: Cal 243; Net Carbs 3.9g; Fat 21g; Protein 9g

Roasted Ham with Radishes

Ingredients for 4 servings
1 lb radishes, halved
Salt and black pepper to taste
1 tbsp cold butter
3 slices deli ham, chopped

Directions and Total Time: approx. 30 minutes
Preheat oven to 375 F. Arrange the radishes on a greased baking sheet. Season with salt and pepper; divide butter and ham on top. Bake for 25 minutes. Serve.

Per serving: Cal 68; Net Carbs 0.5g; Fat 4g; Protein 4g

Green Bean & Mozzarella Roast with Bacon

Ingredients for 4 servings

2 tbsp olive oil
1 tsp onion powder
1 egg, beaten
15 oz fresh green beans
5 tbsp grated mozzarella
4 bacon slices, chopped

Directions and Total Time: approx. 30 minutes

Preheat oven to 350 F and line a baking sheet with parchment paper. In a bowl, mix olive oil, onion and garlic powders, salt, pepper, and egg. Add in green beans and mozzarella; toss to coat. Pour the mixture onto the baking sheet and bake until the green beans brown slightly and cheese melts, 20 minutes. Fry bacon in a skillet until crispy and brown. Remove green beans and divide between serving plates. Top with bacon and serve.

Per serving: Cal 208; Net Carbs 2.6g; Fat 19g; Protein 6g

Cheddar Bacon & Celeriac Bake

Ingredients for 4 servings

6 bacon slices, chopped
3 tbsp butter
3 garlic cloves, minced
3 tbsp almond flour
2 cups coconut cream
1 cup chicken broth
Salt and black pepper to taste
2 lb celeriac, peeled and sliced
2 cups shredded cheddar
¼ cup chopped scallions

Directions and Total Time: approx. 1 hour 30 minutes

Preheat oven to 400 F. Add bacon to a skillet and fry over medium heat until brown and crispy. Spoon onto a plate. Melt butter in the same skillet and sauté garlic for 1 minute. Mix in almond flour and cook for another minute. Whisk in coconut cream, broth, and season with salt and pepper. Simmer for 5 minutes. Spread a layer of the sauce in a greased casserole dish, arrange a layer celeriac on top, cover with more sauce, top with some bacon and cheddar cheese, and scatter scallions on top. Repeat the layering process until the ingredients are exhausted. Bake for 75 minutes. Let rest and serve.

Per serving: Cal 981; Net Carbs 20.5g; Fat 86g; Protein 28g

Chicken Ham with Mini Bell Peppers

Ingredients for 4 servings

12 mini green bell peppers, halved and deseeded
4 slices chicken ham, chopped
1 tbsp chopped parsley
8 oz cream cheese
½ tbsp hot sauce
2 tbsp melted butter
1 cup shredded Gruyere

Directions and Total Time: approx. 30 minutes

Preheat oven to 400 F. Place peppers in a greased baking dish and set aside. In a bowl, combine chicken ham, parsley, cream cheese, hot sauce, and butter. Spoon the mixture into the peppers and sprinkle Gruyere cheese on top. Bake until the cheese melts, 15 minutes. Serve.

Per serving: Cal 408; Net Carbs 4g; Fat 32g; Protein 19g

Crispy Baked Cheese Asparagus

Ingredients for 4 servings

1 cup grated Pecorino Romano cheese
4 slices Serrano ham, chopped
2 lb asparagus, stalks trimmed
¾ cup coconut cream
3 garlic cloves, minced
1 cup crushed pork rinds
1 cup grated mozzarella
½ tsp sweet paprika

Directions and Total Time: approx. 40 minutes

Preheat oven to 400 F. Arrange asparagus on a greased baking dish and pour coconut cream on top. Scatter the garlic on top, season with salt and pepper, top with pork rinds, serrano ham, and sprinkle with Pecorino cheese, mozzarella, and paprika. Bake until the cheese melts and is golden and asparagus tender, 30 minutes. Serve.

Per serving: Cal 361; Net Carbs 15g; Fat 21g; Protein 32g

Creamy Ham & Parsnip Puree

Ingredients for 4 servings

2 lb parsnips, diced
3 tbsp olive oil, divided
2 tsp garlic powder
¾ cup almond milk
4 tbsp heavy cream
4 tbsp butter
6 slices deli ham, chopped
2 tsp freshly chopped oregano

Directions and Total Time: approx. 45 minutes

Preheat oven to 400 F. Spread parsnips on a greased baking sheet, drizzle with 2 tbsp olive oil, and season with salt and pepper. Cover tightly with aluminum foil and bake until the parsnips are tender, 40 minutes. Remove from the oven, take off the foil, and transfer to a bowl. Add in garlic powder, almond milk, heavy cream, and butter. Using an immersion blender, puree the ingredients until smooth. Fold in the ham and sprinkle with oregano.

Per serving: Cal 477; Net Carbs 20g; Fat 30g; Protein 10g

Chili Baked Zucchini Sticks with Aioli

Ingredients for 4 servings

¼ cup Pecorino Romano cheese, shredded
¼ cup pork rind crumbs
1 tsp sweet paprika
Salt and chili pepper to taste
1 cup mayonnaise
Juice from half lemon
2 garlic cloves, minced
3 fresh eggs
2 zucchinis, cut into strips

Directions and Total Time: approx. 25 minutes

Preheat oven to 425 F and line a baking sheet with foil. In a bowl, mix pork rinds, paprika, Pecorino Romano cheese, salt, and chili pepper. Beat the eggs in another bowl. Coat zucchini strips in egg, then in the cheese mixture, and arrange on the sheet. Grease lightly with cooking spray and bake for 15 minutes. Combine in a bowl mayonnaise, lemon juice, and garlic, and gently stir until everything is well incorporated. Serve the strips with aioli.

Per serving: Cal 180; Net Carbs 2g; Fat 14g; Protein 6g

Cauliflower Rice & Bacon Gratin

Ingredients for 4 servings

1 cup canned artichoke hearts, drained and chopped
6 bacon slices, chopped
2 cups cauliflower rice
3 cups baby spinach, chopped
1 garlic clove, minced
1 tbsp olive oil
Salt and black pepper to taste
¼ cup sour cream
8 oz cream cheese, softened
¼ cup grated Parmesan
1 ½ cups grated mozzarella

Directions and Total Time: approx. 30 minutes

Preheat oven to 350 F. Cook bacon in a skillet over medium heat until brown and crispy, 5 minutes. Spoon onto a plate. In a bowl, mix cauli rice, artichokes, spinach, garlic, olive oil, salt, pepper, sour cream, cream cheese, bacon, and half of Parmesan cheese. Spread the mixture into a baking dish and top with the remaining Parmesan and mozzarella cheeses. Bake 15 minutes. Serve.

Per serving: Cal 500; Net Carbs 5.3g; Fat 37g; Protein 28g

Crunchy Rutabaga Puffs

Ingredients for 4 servings

1 rutabaga, peeled and diced
2 tbsp melted butter
½ oz goat cheese
¼ cup ground pork rinds

Directions and Total Time: approx. 35 minutes

Preheat oven to 400 F and spread rutabaga on a baking sheet. Season with salt, pepper, and drizzle with the butter. Bake until tender, 15 minutes. Transfer to a bowl. Allow cooling and add in goat cheese. Using a fork, mash and mix the ingredients. Pour the pork rinds onto a plate. Mold 1-inch balls out of the rutabaga mixture and roll properly in the rinds while pressing gently to stick. Place in the same baking sheet and bake for 10 minutes until golden.

Per serving: Cal 129; Net Carbs 5.9g; Fat 8g; Protein 3g

Crispy Pancetta & Butternut Squash Roast

Ingredients for 4 servings

2 butternut squash, cubed

1 tsp turmeric powder

½ tsp garlic powder

8 pancetta slices, chopped

2 tbsp olive oil

1 tbsp chopped cilantro,

Directions and Total Time: approx. 30 minutes

Preheat oven to 425 F. In a bowl, add butternut squash, salt, pepper, turmeric, garlic powder, pancetta, and olive oil. Toss until well-coated. Spread the mixture onto a greased baking sheet and roast for 10-15 minutes. Transfer the veggies to a bowl and garnish with cilantro to serve.

Per serving: Cal 148; Net Carbs 6.4g; Fat 10g; Protein 6g

Simple Stuffed Eggs with Mayonnaise

Ingredients for 6 servings

6 eggs

1 tbsp green tabasco

¼ cup mayonnaise

2 tbsp black olives, sliced

Directions and Total Time: approx. 30 minutes

Place eggs in a saucepan and cover with salted water. Boil for 10 minutes. Place the eggs in an ice bath and let cool. Peel and slice in half lengthwise. Scoop out the yolks to a bowl; mash with a fork. Whisk together the tabasco, mayonnaise, mashed yolks, and salt, in a bowl. Spoon this mixture into egg white. Garnish with olive slices to serve.

Per serving: Cal 178; Net Carbs: 5g; Fat: 17g; Protein: 6g

Cheesy Pork Rind Bread

Ingredients for 4 servings

¼ cup grated Pecorino Romano cheese

8 oz cream cheese

2 cups grated mozzarella

1 tbsp baking powder

1 cup crushed pork rinds

3 large eggs

1 tbsp Italian mixed herbs

Directions and Total Time: approx. 30 minutes

Preheat oven to 375 F and line a baking sheet with parchment paper. Microwave cream and mozzarella cheeses for 1 minute or until melted. Whisk in baking powder, pork rinds, eggs, Pecorino cheese, and mixed herbs. Spread the mixture in the baking sheet and bake for 20 minutes until lightly brown. Let cool, slice and serve.

Per serving: Cal 437; Net Carbs 3.2g; Fat 23g; Protein 32g

Savory Lime Fried Artichokes

Ingredients for 4 servings

12 fresh baby artichokes
2 tbsp lime juice
2 tbsp olive oil
Salt to taste

Directions and Total Time: approx. 20 minutes

Slice artichokes vertically into narrow wedges. Drain on paper towels before frying. Heat olive oil in a skillet. Fry the artichokes until browned and crispy. Drain excess oil on paper towels. Sprinkle with salt and lime juice.

Per serving: Cal 35; Net Carbs: 2.9g; Fat: 2.4g; Protein: 2g

Rosemary Cheese Chips with Guacamole

Ingredients for 4 servings

1 tbsp rosemary
1 cup Grana Padano, grated
¼ tsp sweet paprika
¼ tsp garlic powder
2 avocados, pitted and scooped
1 tomato, chopped

Directions and Total Time: approx. 20 minutes

Preheat oven to 350 F and line a baking sheet with parchment paper. Mix Grana Padano cheese, paprika, rosemary, and garlic powder evenly. Spoon 6-8 teaspoons on the baking sheet creating spaces between each mound.; flatten mounds. Bake for 5 minutes, cool, and remove to a plate. To make the guacamole, mash avocado, with a fork in a bowl, add in tomato and continue to mash until mostly smooth. Season with salt. Serve crackers with guacamole.

Per serving: Cal 229; Net Carbs 2g; Fat 20g; Protein 10g

Parmesan Green Bean Crisps

Ingredients for 6 servings

¼ cup Parmesan, shredded
¼ cup pork rind crumbs
1 tsp minced garlic
2 eggs
1 lb green beans
Salt and black pepper to taste

Directions and Total Time: approx. 30 minutes

Preheat oven to 425 F and line two baking sheets with foil. Mix Parmesan cheese, pork rinds, garlic, salt, and pepper in a bowl. Beat the eggs in another bowl. Coat green beans in eggs, then cheese mixture and arrange evenly on the baking sheets. Grease lightly with cooking spray and bake for 15 minutes. Transfer to a wire rack to cool. Serve.

Per serving: Cal 210; Net Carbs 3g; Fat 19g; Protein 5g

Paprika & Dill Deviled Eggs

Ingredients for 4 servings

1 tsp dill, chopped
8 large eggs
3 cups water
3 tbsp sriracha sauce
4 tbsp mayonnaise
¼ tsp sweet paprika

Directions and Total Time: approx. 20 minutes

Bring eggs to boil in salted water, reduce the heat, and simmer for 10 minutes. Transfer to an ice water bath, let cool completely and peel the shells. Slice the eggs in half height wise and empty the yolks into a bowl. Smash with a fork and mix in sriracha sauce, mayonnaise, and half of the paprika until smooth. Spoon filling into a piping bag and fill the egg whites to be slightly above the brim. Garnish with remaining paprika and dill and serve immediately.

Per serving: Cal 195; Net Carbs 1g; Fat 19g; Protein 4g

Cheese & Garlic Crackers

Ingredients for 6 servings

1 ¼ cups Pecorino Romano cheese, grated
1 ¼ cups coconut flour
Salt and black pepper to taste
1 tsp garlic powder
¼ cup ghee
¼ tsp sweet paprika
½ cup heavy cream

Directions and Total Time: approx. 30 minutes

Preheat oven to 350 F. Mix flour, Pecorino Romano cheese, salt, pepper, garlic and paprika in a bowl. Add in ghee and mix well. Top with heavy cream and mix again until a thick mixture has formed. Cover the dough with plastic wrap. Use a rolling pin to spread out the dough into a light rectangle. Cut into cracker squares and arrange them on a baking sheet. Bake for 20 minutes.

Per serving: Cal 115; Net Carbs 0.7g; Fat 3g; Protein 5g

Cheesy Chicken Wraps

Ingredients for 8 servings

¼ tsp garlic powder
8 ounces fontina cheese
8 raw chicken tenders
8 prosciutto slices

Directions and Total Time: approx. 20 minutes

Pound chicken until half an inch thick. Season with garlic powder. Cut fontina cheese into 8 strips. Place a slice of prosciutto on a flat surface. Place one chicken tender on top. Top with a fontina strip. Roll the chicken and secure with skewers. Grill the wraps for 3 minutes per side.

Per serving: Cal 174; Net Carbs: 0.7g; Fat: 10g; Protein: 17g

Baked Chorizo with Cottage Cheese

Ingredients for 6 servings
7 oz Spanish chorizo, sliced
4 oz cottage cheese, pureed
¼ cup chopped parsley
Directions and Total Time: approx. 30 minutes
Preheat the oven to 325 F. Line a baking dish with waxed paper. Bake the chorizo for 15 minutes until crispy. Remove from the oven and let cool. Arrange on a serving platter. Top each slice with cottage cheese and parsley.
Per serving: Cal 172; Net Carbs: 0.2g; Fat: 13g; Protein: 5g

Goat Cheese Stuffed Peppers

Ingredients for 8 servings
8 canned roasted piquillo peppers
3 slices prosciutto, cut into thin slices
2 tbsp olive oil
8 ounces goat cheese
3 tbsp heavy cream
3 tbsp chopped parsley
½ tsp minced garlic
1 tbsp chopped mint
Directions and Total Time: approx. 15 minutes
Combine goat cheese, heavy cream, parsley, garlic, and mint in a bowl. Place the mixture in a freezer bag, press down and squeeze, and cut off the bottom. Drain and deseed the peppers. Squeeze about 2 tbsp of the filling into each pepper. Wrap a prosciutto slice onto each pepper. Secure with toothpicks. Arrange them on a serving platter. Sprinkle the olive oil and vinegar over.
Per serving: Cal 110; Net Carbs 2.5g; Fat 9g; Protein 6g

DESSERTS

Lemon Curd Tarts

Ingredients for 4 servings
For the crust:
¼ cup swerve confectioner's sugar
1 ½ cups almond flour
½ tsp salt
¼ cup unsalted butter, melted
1 large egg
For the filling:
½ cup swerve confectioner's sugar
4 tbsp salted butter
½ lemon, zested and juiced
3 large eggs
Directions and Total Time: approx. 25 min + chilling time
Preheat oven to 350 F and lightly grease 4 (2x12-inch) mini tart tins with cooking spray. In a food processor, blend flour, swerve, salt, butter, and egg. Divide and spread the dough in the tins and press. Bake for 15 minutes. For the filling, melt butter in a pot over medium heat, take off the heat and quickly mix in swerve, lemon zest, and lemon juice until smooth. Whisk in eggs and return the pot to low heat. Cook with continuous stirring until thick. Pour the filling into the crust, gently tap on a flat surface to release air bubbles and chill in the refrigerator for at least 1 hour.
Per serving: Cal 213; Net Carbs 2g; Fat 20g; Protein 7g

Fresh Berry Tarts

Ingredients for 4 servings
For the crust:
6 tbsp butter, melted
2 cups almond flour
1/3 cup xylitol
1 tsp cinnamon powder
For the filling:
1 cup coconut cream
2 cups frozen berries
Swerve confectioner's sugar for topping
Directions and Total Time: approx. 20 min + chilling time
Preheat oven to 350 F and lightly grease 4 (2x12-inch) mini tart tins with cooking spray. In a food processor, blend butter, flour, xylitol, and cinnamon. Divide and spread the dough in the tart tins and bake for 15 minutes.
Remove crust from oven and let cool. Divide the coconut cream into the tart crusts and divide the berries on top. Garnish with some swerve sugar and enjoy.
Per serving: Cal 246; Net Carbs 5.5g; Fat 21g; Protein 5g

Peanut Butter Mousse

Ingredients for 4 servings
½ cup heavy cream
4 oz softened cream cheese
¼ cup smooth peanut butter
¼ cup xylitol
½ tsp vanilla extract

Directions and Total Time: approx. 10 minutes
Whip ½ cup of heavy cream in a bowl using an electric mixer until stiff peaks hole; set aside. In another bowl, beat cream cheese and peanut butter until creamy and smooth. Mix in xylitol and vanilla extract until well combined. Gradually, fold in the cream mixture until well combined. If too thick, fold in 2 tbsp of the reserved heavy cream. Spoon the mousse into dessert glasses and serve.

Per serving: Cal 231; Net Carbs 5g; Fat 21g; Protein 6.2g

Strawberry Cheesecake Tart

Ingredients for 4 servings
For the crust:
6 tbsp butter, melted
2 cups almond flour
1/3 cup xylitol
1 tsp cinnamon powder
For the filling:
¼ cup swerve confectioner's sugar
1 cup softened cream cheese
½ cup heavy cream
1 tsp vanilla extract
1 cup halved strawberries

Directions and Total Time: approx. 25 min + chilling time
Preheat oven to 350 F and grease a round baking pan. In a food processor, blend butter, flour, xylitol, and cinnamon until the dough mixture resembles ball-like shape. Stretch out the dough in the pan covering the sides; with a fork stab the bottom of the crust. Bake for 15 minutes. Remove the crust after cooking and let cool. In a bowl, whisk cheese, heavy cream, swerve, and vanilla extract. Pour the filling into the crust, gently tap on a flat surface to release air bubbles and refrigerate for 1 hour. Remove tart from the fridge, and top with strawberries.

Per serving: Cal 401; Net Carbs 6g; Fat 33g; Protein 5g

Simple Chocolate Tart

Ingredients for 4 servings

For the crust:
1 1/3 cups almond flour
1 ½ tsp coconut flour
¼ cup swerve sugar
1 ½ tsp cold water
3 tbsp cold butter

For the filling:
4 oz heavy cream
4 oz dark chocolate chips
1/3 cup erythritol

Directions and Total Time: approx. 25 min + chilling time

Preheat oven to 350 F. In a food processor, blend almond and coconut flours, swerve, water, and butter until smooth. Spread the dough in a greased round baking pan and bake for 15 minutes; let cool. For the filling, heat heavy cream and chocolate chips in a pot over medium heat until chocolate melts; whisk in erythritol. Pour the filling into the crust, gently tap on a flat surface to release air bubbles and chill for 1 hour. Remove from the fridge, and serve.

Per serving: Cal 177; Net Carbs 1g; Fat 19g; Protein 3g

Rhubarb Tart

Ingredients for 6 servings

For the crust:
6 oz almond flour
1/3 cup swerve sugar
3 oz butter, melted
2 tbsp shredded coconut

For the rhubarb filling:
4 ¼ oz butter, softened
½ cup swerve sugar
¾ cups almond flour
1 cup almond milk
3 eggs
1 tsp vanilla extract
7 oz rhubarb, spiralized

Directions and Total Time: approx. 70 minutes

Preheat oven to 350 F. In a food processor, blend the flour, swerve, butter, and coconut. Spread the dough in a greased tart tin and bake in the oven for 13 minutes; let cool. For the filling, in a bowl, whisk butter, swerve, flour, almond milk, eggs, and vanilla. Pour the filling into the crust, gently tap on a flat surface to release air bubbles and press rhubarb spirals into the filling. Bake further for 35 minutes until the filling sets. Remove, let cool and serve.

Per serving: Cal 478; Net Carbs 7.2g; Fat 33g; Protein 14g

Mixed Berry Custard Pots

Ingredients for 4 servings

6 egg yolks
½ cup almond milk
1 tsp vanilla extract
1 tsp swerve sugar
1 cup mixed berries, chopped

Directions and Total Time: approx. 15 minutes

In a metal bowl, whisk yolks, milk, vanilla, and swerve until smooth. Bring some water to a boil over medium heat and place the bowl over the water. Whisk the mixture constantly until thickened, 5 minutes or until reached 140 F. Take the bowl off the water and mix in the berries. Divide the custard between 4 dessert cups and enjoy.

Per serving: Cal 176; Net Carbs 6.4g; Fat 14g; Protein 4.9g

Swiss Mascarpone Mousse with Chocolate

Ingredients for 6 servings

For the mascarpone chocolate mousse:

8 oz mascarpone cheese
8 oz heavy cream
4 tbsp cocoa powder
4 tbsp xylitol

For the vanilla mousse:

3.5 oz cream cheese
3.5 oz heavy cream
1 tsp vanilla extract
2 tbsp xylitol

Directions and Total Time: approx. 15 minutes

In a bowl using and electric mixer, beat mascarpone cheese, heavy cream, cocoa, and xylitol until creamy. Do not over mix, however. In another bowl, whisk all vanilla mousse ingredients until smooth and creamy. Gradually fold vanilla mousse mixture into the mascarpone one until well incorporated. Spoon into dessert cups and serve.

Per serving: Cal 412; Net Carbs 5.9g; Fat 32g; Protein 8g

Lemon Curd Mousse with Caramel Nuts

Ingredients for 4 servings

For the mousse:

8 oz cream cheese

1 cup cold heavy cream

1 tsp vanilla extract

¼ cup swerve sugar

½ lemon, juiced

For the caramel nuts:

2/3 cup swerve brown sugar

A pinch salt

1 cup mixed nuts, chopped

Directions and Total Time: approx. 10 min + chilling time

In a stand mixer, beat cream cheese and heavy cream until creamy. Add vanilla, swerve, and lemon juice until smooth. Divide the mixture between 4 dessert cups, cover with plastic wrap and refrigerate for at least 2 hours.

For the caramel nuts:

Add swerve sugar to a large skillet and cook over medium heat with frequent stirring until melted and golden brown. Mix in water, salt, and cook further until syrupy and slightly thickened. Turn the heat off and quickly mix in the nuts until well coated in the caramel; let sit for 5 minutes or until golden. Remove the mousse from the fridge and top with the caramel nuts. Serve immediately.

Per serving: Cal 516; Net Carbs 8g; Fat 52.7g; Protein 7.3g

Tasty Strawberry Mousse

Ingredients for 4 servings

12 fresh strawberries, hulled + extra for topping

2 tbsp swerve sugar

½ cup softened cream cheese

1 cup heavy whipping cream

Directions and Total Time: approx. 10 min + chilling time

In a food processor, blend strawberries and swerve until smooth. Add cream cheese and process until smooth. Pour in the heavy cream and blend smoothly too. Divide the mousse into 4 medium glasses and refrigerate for 1 hour. Top with some strawberries when ready to serve.

Per serving: Cal 204; Net Carbs 4.7g; Fat 19.8g; Protein 3g

Blackberry Chocolate Mousse Pots

Ingredients for 4 servings
½ cup swerve confectioner's sugar
2 ½ cups unsweetened dark chocolate, melted
3 cups heavy cream
½ tsp vanilla extract
½ cup blackberries, chopped
Some blackberries for topping

Directions and Total Time: approx. 10 min + chilling time
In a stand mixer, beat heavy cream and swerve sugar until creamy. Add dark chocolate and vanilla extract, and mix until smoothly combined. Fold in blackberries until well distributed. Divide the mixture between 4 dessert cups, cover with plastic wrap and refrigerate for 2 hours. from fridge, garnish with blackberries and serve immediately.

Per serving: Cal 312; Net Carbs 2.6g; Fat 33g; Protein 1.9g

White Chocolate Mousse

Ingredients for 4 servings
6 oz unsweetened white chocolate, chopped
1 ½ cups cold heavy cream

Directions and Total Time: approx. 10 min + chilling time
Add white chocolate and ½ cup of heavy cream to a microwave-safe bowl. Microwave until melted, frequently stirring, for 60 seconds. Remove from the microwave and let cool at room temperature. Pour the mixture into a stand mixer and whisk with the remaining heavy cream until soft peaks form. Divide the mousse between 4 dessert cups, chill for at least 2 hours and serve.

Per serving: Cal 155; Net Carbs 1.3g; Fat 16.7g; Protein 3g

APPENDIX : RECIPES INDEX

CPSIA information can be obtained
at www.ICGtesting.com
Printed in the USA
BVHW060443120521
607043BV00007B/1697

9 781802 445831